BE YOUR OWN
DETECTIVE

BE YOUR OWN
DETECTIVE

Greg Fallis and Ruth Greenberg

M. EVANS AND COMPANY, INC.   **NEW YORK**

M. Evans and Company, Inc.
216 East 49th Street
New York, New York 10017

ISBN 0-87131-872-5

Designed and typeset by Rik Lain Schell

Printed in the United States of America

9 8 7 6 5 4 3 2 1

Contents

Acknowledgments

The authors would like to express their sincere appreciation to Susannah, without whom this would not have been possible.

This book is dedicated to:

Frank H., good as family, a quick and liberal hand at the bottle and always game for outlandish enterprise. I have no higher praise.

Anita G., the only northern light I saw on those surreal road shows to the wilds of Maine.

Bruce S., who kept me out of almost as much trouble as he got me into.

And especially to Betsy K., for reasons too numerous to catalog.

G.F.

And to Thurgood Marshall, Ted Kennedy, Joe Biden, David Garfunkel, and my mom and dad. They know why.

R.G.

Authors' Note

The incidents and cases presented in this book are based on actual events. To protect the people involved, however, some of the facts and circumstances have been altered or fictionalized. Some examples are composites of more than one case.

PREFACE TO THE SECOND EDITION

It's been nearly a decade since Ruth Greenberg and I first put our collective heads together and pounded out *Be Your Own Detective*. Our original intent in writing the book was both somewhat political and somewhat mercenary. We wanted to make some of the more common investigative techniques available to folks who couldn't afford the services of a professional private investigator. We wanted to teach folks how to do what real investigators do. And we wanted to make a quick buck while doing it.

I think we were both surprised, however, at the response to the book. We began the process in order to teach others, but over the years I think we've both learned something as well.

One of the things I learned was that learning transforms you. It changes the way you perceive yourself. I occasionally received letters from readers, folks who had used some of the techniques and ideas from *Be Your Own Detective*. Several of the letter writers mentioned how they had been affected by learning to use the techniques and actually putting them into practice. They didn't always get the results they'd wanted, but simply using their newfound skills changed the way they saw themselves. Take, for example, the woman who decided she needed to investigate her lover. The reasons she made that decision, and what she discovered, are irrelevant. What is relevant is that before she made the decision she thought of herself as an ordinary person. Afterwards, however, she saw herself in a different light. She was a woman who had taken on a difficult task and had done it—and done it rather well. She felt she'd discovered a new self. She wasn't universally happy with her new self—she didn't particularly like the fact that she was the sort of person who would tail her lover—but she liked the fact that she felt capable of doing whatever she needed to do to look out for herself.

I could empathize with her situation. I still recall the very first time I had to go to the house of a stranger, knock on the door, and ask a series of terribly nosy questions of the person who answered. It was an intimidating task. It was my job, though, so I did it. Eventually, it became second nature to me. But on that day I began to change. I went from being a normal person who minded his own business to a person who felt totally at ease asking total strangers with the intimate details of their private lives. Like the woman who investigated her lover, I wasn't always pleased about the person I had become. I discovered aspects of my personality that troubled and offended me. On the other hand, I was proud of my skill as an investigator.

Why are we telling you this? As a warning. Ruth and I will show you how to be your own detective. But you should be aware that when you investigate others, you also investigate yourself.

G.F.

INTRODUCTION

I'm a criminal lawyer. I know what detectives do. And I know you can learn to do it, too.

Almost a thousand people accused of crimes have come to me for help. Some were innocent. Most were guilty.

The innocent needed me to find out what really happened. The guilty wanted me to get them off the hook. For both of these jobs, I needed a detective.

For a long time, Greg Fallis was the man for the job. I found the law, he found the facts. I knew the library and the courtroom, he knew the courtroom and the world. We were a team. Sometimes we won.

Sometimes after court was over for the day, we'd sit around drinking and talking. And Greg would tell stories about his work, some of the same stories he tells here. It was a world far different from the courtroom. I wanted to know it. I thought it would make me a better lawyer. I asked him to teach me, and he agreed.

At first I went with him on the job. I did what he said. I learned a lot. I got the basic tools.

It was tough going, those nights in smoke-filled bars, those days in line at the Department of Motor Vehicles. Sometimes I had to wear a down jacket, sometimes a suit, stockings, and pearls. I looked at blood, at broken boards, and at thousands of dull documents. I smelled of burned buildings and leftover fried chicken. I talked to many men, women, and children, and I learned a trade far different from my own.

So can you.

To guide you, I've added some stories from own experience along the way. And to guard you from legal peril, I've included a chapter on the detective and the law.

Before you begin, two very important warnings from those years as a criminal lawyer:

1. Sometimes you'll never know what really happened.

In police shows, there's almost always a solution. In real life, most police like to think there's a solution. That way someone goes to jail, and we all feel safe.

But the true detective knows sometimes you can't know. There is a limit to this art. Know your limit.

2. Sometimes you'll find out what really happened.

Let's imagine a forty-year-old alcoholic burglar, female, who has a fourteen-year-old retarded child confined to a wheelchair. The burglar moves in with a fellow who is fond of children. So fond that one night he has sex with the crippled girl, who bears a child. The fellow goes to jail for statutory rape, and the baby is adopted by a nice family who loves her. Do you want to tell her who her birth parents are?

Remember what happened when Eve picked the apple and when Pandora opened the box. Not all knowledge is good.

A talk show host, hearing about this book, asked us, "Aren't you worried that when you teach people how to do these things they'll get themselves into trouble? Maybe commit crimes? Aren't you afraid of what people will do with the information?"

The simple answer is no. I'm sworn to uphold the Constitution and the Constitution upholds our right to speak freely. I don't think a person can have too much information.

This book provides access to skills and techniques that you can use for good or evil. You can operate within or outside the law. As a member in good standing of the bar, I advise you to obey the law. As to good or evil, because I am a member of the bar, I don't advise.

You can learn to be your own detective. You can eat the apple; you can open the box. But be careful. Once you know, you can't forget.

R.G.

I'm going to tell you how to do the things detectives do. *Real* detectives, not the ones you see on television or read about in novels. Real-life detective work can't be done in an hour, nor can it be arranged around commercial breaks. It's often tough, lonely work; it's difficult to do well and frequently unappreciated.

But if you want to know how to do it, I'll teach you. I'll tell you how to find people, how to watch them and follow them, how to get them to talk to you and tell you the things you want to know. I'll tell you how to develop sources of information and how to work your way through the maze of official files. I'll tell you about the ways real investigators use technology, and what technology is available—and useful—to amateurs.

I'll teach you what I've learned, the techniques I've acquired through experience and from other detectives. I'll give you examples of how those techniques are used. I'll tell you what has worked for me. I'll even tell you about the things that haven't worked.

I'll let you in the back door of the detective's world.

But as you read this book and examine the techniques, try to think of other ways to achieve the same results. Don't accept what I tell you as gospel; what you read here are merely suggestions based on what has worked for me and for others in the same profession. Ask yourself how the techniques could be adapted to suit your own personality. There are very few rules in detective work, but there is one overriding precept: question everything.

That's what being a detective is all about, after all.

When I first began to work as a detective, I was immediately overwhelmed. There was so much I didn't know. My first assignment involved finding witnesses to a hit-and-run accident that had taken place on a thinly populated road. It was a simple assignment on the face of it. A few weeks earlier, a car had jammed on its brakes, causing a motorcycle to smash into it from behind. The motorcycle was demolished, and the rider was thrown onto the trunk of the car. When the driver of the car sped off, the badly injured motorcyclist rolled off the trunk and into a ditch.

All I had to do was find somebody who saw it happen. It sounded easy—and exciting.

My first task was to go to the scene of the accident. When I got there, my excitement dimmed somewhat. There were only a few houses within half a mile of the accident site. Not a lot of potential witnesses. Hoping for the best, I went to the closest house and knocked on the door. Nobody answered. I knew somebody was in the house, though—the television was playing loudly. I knocked louder and with the same result. Nothing.

Already I was stumped. Should I go around to the back door and try again? The back door was behind a chain-link fence, but the gate was open. Would that be trespassing? Should I peek in the windows? Was that legal? Maybe I should just leave and come back later. Maybe the person in the house had had an accident and was unable to come to the door. Maybe they were unconscious. Maybe they were dead. Maybe they'd been murdered by the hit-and-run driver. I pounded on the door wildly with my fist, and a very pleasant and very deaf old woman eventually answered the door. No, she hadn't seen anything on the night in question. Plainly, she hadn't *heard* anything.

It was the same at the other houses. None of the others were actually hearing impaired, but they might as well have been stone deaf and blind as the sailor Pew. Nobody had seen or heard a thing.

Again, I was stumped. I couldn't think of anything else to do. I felt like a failure. So I called another detective and asked for suggestions. "Did you put an ad in the paper asking for witnesses?" she asked. "Have you checked body shops to see if anybody had any repairs done consistent with the accident? Have you gone to the scene at the same time as the accident and written down the license numbers of cars driving by?"

And, of course, I hadn't done any of those things.

"Then get off your butt and get out there," she said.

And I got off my butt. I got out there, and I found three witnesses. All I'd needed was somebody to give me a few ideas.

That's what I'm going to do for you. I'll teach you the basic techniques; I'll give you a few ideas. But in order for them to work, you'll have to get off your butt and get out there. Like I said earlier—that's what the job is all about.

G.F.

Greg arrives in town, one he's never been in before. He didn't expect to be there, so he has no map. It's getting dark. He doesn't know anybody in town, and he doesn't have directions to where he's going. All he knows is that he's got to find a man who works in a bar near the railroad.

As if guided by an invisible hand, he drives almost directly to the bar and is soon drinking a long-neck Bud and talking to the man.

Greg never asks for directions. But he always seems to know where to find a decent meal, or a gas station, or a killer bar.

How does he do it? How was he able to find his way around Eulonia, Georgia, without a map? I finally asked him how.

"Luck," he said. "I have good luck."

It takes luck to be a good detective. And it takes practice, because in this business you often make your own luck.

All other things being equal, I always hire an experienced detective. All towns are not alike, but after you've visited hundreds of new towns, you know where the train tracks are and where a bar will be. And after a thousand new towns, you forget you ever had to learn that, and you call yourself lucky. Just lucky.

When I have a child, I'll teach her to be a detective. I'll take her for long rides in the car and ask her, "Can you show Mommy and Daddy how to get home?" I'll take her for a walk and, afterwards, ask her, "Tell me what you saw." I'll teach her to pay attention from a very early age. That's what Greg's parents did.

I understand that tiny gumshoes can be bronzed.

R.G.

Chapter 1

WHAT IT TAKES

What does it take to be a good detective? Novels and movies would have you believe all it takes is broad shoulders and a thick skull. Or a mind like a computer, or just a trench coat and a gun.

Real life, as always, is both more mundane and more complex.

What it really takes to be a detective—a *good* detective—is a peculiar blend of talents and attitudes. This isn't a quality unique to detectives. The same could be said of the practitioners of almost any field—surgeons, mechanics, architects. Even mass murderers. If you have the potential, you can learn the necessary skills.

In detective work *what* you are is often less important than *who* you are. In many ways, gender, race, physical ability, and such are irrelevant. Those factors can be either a liability or an asset. It all depends on the circumstance and *the person*.

Let me deal with the gender issue right away. Throughout this book I'll refer to the detective as *he*. I don't do this because men are better detectives. I do it because it's practical, and the only gender-neutral pronoun in the English language is *it* (and I have an old-fashioned dislike of inclusive terms like *he/she* or *s/he*). But, again, don't make the mistake of assuming all good detectives are men.

I know a detective who specializes in helping to defend people accused of murder, people charged with the most savage and vicious acts imaginable. Murder is serious business; only the best detectives are asked to work on such cases. This detective is about five feet two, weighs maybe a hundred and ten pounds, and is the mother of two daughters.

I'll repeat myself. *Who* you are—the type of person you are—is more important than *what* you are. You can have shoulders like Superman and a brain like Albert Einstein, but if you don't know what to do with them, you might as well stay in bed.

In this chapter I'm going to tell you what it takes to be a detective; in later chapters I'll tell you what to do with that knowledge. Whether or not you put those skills to use is up to you.

I've divided the criteria of a good detective among four categories:

1. Intellectual
2. Social
3. Emotional
4. Physical

These categories are interrelated. They bleed into each other, which is how it should be. The detective craft is saturated with ambiguity.

THE INTELLECTUAL QUALITIES

You needn't be Sherlock Holmes to be a good detective. While intelligence is important, this isn't rocket science and a stratospheric IQ isn't a prerequisite. Still, the craft does make certain intellectual demands. A good detective needs:

- Street sense
- Analytic ability

 • Curiosity
 • Tangential knowledge

You already have each of these qualities to some extent, probably to a greater degree than you realize. You only need to become more aware of them in order to put them to use.

Street Sense

Street sense is an intuitive understanding of the way the world works and how people move through it. It's a feeling you develop. Like a lot of intuitive processes, street sense can be developed and, once developed, refined. The more time you spend on the street and the more attention you pay to detail, the sharper your street sense will become.

Once I was training a new investigator, helping him find a witness to a drug-related assault. We'd learned the witness often slept in the hallway of a certain seedy tenement. As we entered a back stairwell of the building, we interrupted four men involved in a drug sale. Although no drugs, weapons, or money were in plain view, it was clear what was taking place. At least it was clear to me. The new investigator had no idea what we'd walked into. He knew *something* was wrong; he felt the tension. And he stopped dead still. It was the worst thing he could have done.

Had we just nodded and continued up the stairs, we would almost certainly have been ignored. But by stopping, he threw sand in the system. A drug sale is a volatile situation. Each of the parties involved has to control his suspicion of the others long enough to make the exchange. Nobody wants to see strangers blundering onto the scene. Strangers mean trouble. Everybody has to assume a stranger works for the other side. Or for the police.

We all stood very still for a long moment. Then I patted my pockets, turned to the other investigator, and said I thought I'd dropped my car keys outside. I suggested we go look for them. I hadn't lost my keys, of course. I just wanted an excuse to get the hell out of there.

The new investigator's street sense was developed enough to know there was danger, but not developed enough to know why. When he asked how *I* knew, I found it difficult to answer. There was something about the posture of the people in the stairwell, about the degree of intensity in the way they watched each other, about the aggressive caution in their eyes when we barged in. I just *knew*.

The only way you can sharpen your street sense is to spend time on the streets. This doesn't mean you need to hang out with drug dealers. It just means you need to go out there and look. Take walks and pay attention to the people you see. What are they doing? How do they carry themselves? What information can you discern from what you see?

Go to a bar, even if you don't drink. Order a beer (or a club soda with a twist of lime—the bartender will think you're on the wagon) and quietly look around. Notice how the people interact. Can you identify the regulars? How?

Pay attention. I'll repeat those words frequently. Pay attention to everything. You can sort out what matters later.

Analytic Ability

A detective uses his analytic powers to solve problems. He takes seemingly unconnected bits of information and fits them together to form a plausible and logical account of events. It takes an agile mind, one capable of looking at a set of facts from a variety of perspectives and willing to view those facts objectively.

A good detective sees connections where other people wouldn't. The connections are always there; nothing happens in a vacuum. Your job is to find those connections.

Curiosity

As we all know, curiosity killed the cat. But a cat wouldn't be a cat without it, nor would a detective be a detective. Every good detective I know is intensely curious. It's not always an attractive quality and, if not kept under control, it can get you or your client in trouble. There are questions that need not be asked, answers that need not be sought.

I had a client who was charged with a major felony, a crime he claimed he hadn't committed. The client said he was in Cape Cod on the weekend of the crime, but he couldn't recall the name of the motel he had stayed in.

I confess I was skeptical—those sorts of alibis rarely pan out. But I wasn't so skeptical that I was willing to pass up a chance to spend some time on the Cape. So I went to the village the client had claimed he'd visited, nosed around, and, to my surprise, I found the motel he'd stayed in. I even talked the manager into giving me a copy of the motel registration ticket.

The only problem was the time he'd checked in. It was possible—just barely, but still possible—that he could have committed the crime and managed to drive to Cape Cod, arriving at the motel by the time noted on the register. He would have had to have driven like a madman and violated every speed law in existence, but everybody drives that way in Massachusetts.

I probably didn't need to do anything more. The motel registration most likely would have been sufficient to establish reasonable doubt before a jury. But I was curious. I still had questions. I had to see if I could find witnesses to place the client in that village *before* he checked into the motel, to establish beyond any doubt that he couldn't have committed the crime.

And I did. In a bar near the motel, I found three people who could swear that the client was at that bar prior to checking into the motel—three people who could clear him of the crime. But we couldn't use them as witnesses. Why? Because the client was in the bar selling drugs to those witnesses.

Sometimes you can better serve your client (or yourself) by not asking questions, by not looking for all the answers. It seems unnatural, like trying to teach a cat not to hunt, but at times it must be so.

Tangential Knowledge

Tangential knowledge is what you call those odd bits of information you collect over the years, information with seemingly little practical use. Baseball statistics, perhaps, or a knowledge of plate tectonics, or the nesting habits of wrens. Other than game-show contestants and writers, detectives are probably the only people in the world who find a use for such information.

Why does a detective need a large fund of tangential information? Because you never know what sort of information might be important.

I needed to interview a doctor, a trauma specialist, who'd examined the victim of an assault. I met him during a quiet period at the emergency room. But he didn't want to speak with me. He was relaxing, reading a book.

A book. One man had been badly injured and another was facing a long prison term, and this guy was too busy to talk to me because he was *reading a book*. Then I saw the title of the book: it was the play *Juno and the Paycock*, by Sean O'Casey. The doctor was an amateur thespian.

So instead of asking him about the case, I talked to him about the play. I don't know much about the theater, but I know a little about Irish history. (The play takes place during the Anglo-Irish War.) For the next half hour, we discussed Ireland and the Irish. Then he told me everything I wanted to know about the case.

There's no way I could have known how to prepare for that interview. I was just lucky I knew something the doctor was interested in. It doesn't always work so well. There have been a lot of interviews I might have gotten if I'd known anything about auto mechanics.

You know similar sorts of things. Maybe not about the history of Ireland, but you *know* things: how to tile a bathroom, where to find good fresh produce, how a barometer works.

Build on that knowledge. Read a lot. It doesn't matter what, just read. Anything. Science fiction, gothic novels, ingredient labels, any words in a row. And listen to other people, even if they're dull. They know things, too, and are willing to share it with you. In fact, dull people *insist* on sharing it. Read, listen, and pay attention.

Most of what you learn will never be useful. It's extremely unlikely you'll ever need to be able to discuss coracles, or the feeding habits of smallmouth bass, or the rules of bocce ball.

But you might.

THE SOCIAL QUALITIES

When I say a good detective needs good social skills I don't mean he needs to be able to tell a soup spoon from a salad fork, although that never hurts. What I mean is that the ability to communicate effectively, to establish a quick rapport, and to appear comfortable in almost any circumstance are critical skills.

A good detective needs:

1. Good listening skills
2. The ability to put others at ease
3. Good acting skills
4. The ability to speak at the level of your audience
5. An understanding of body language

I'll discuss these skills in more detail later in the book. But it's important to note them now. Trying to do business without these skills is like trying to eat your soup with a salad fork.

A really good detective can fit into almost any social circumstance, even unfamiliar ones. How? By staying calm, acting as if you belong, and paying attention.

I know an investigator who tailed a subject to a Catholic church one Sunday morning. It was a big church with a lot of exits, and the investigator was afraid his subject would be able to slip out a side door when the mass was over. He also wanted to know if the subject was meeting somebody in the church.

So he followed the man in. Not such a big deal, except that the investigator is Jewish. Once inside the church, he was surrounded by an alien culture. He didn't know when to stand up, when to sit down, when to kneel. He didn't know the hymns or the responses to the litany, didn't even know what a litany was. He was familiar with the concept of communion, but had no idea what a communion wafer looked like, how it was taken, or if it could be avoided without drawing attention to oneself. He was absolutely lost.

But he stayed calm, smiled politely, and paid attention to the people around him. He stood up when they did, knelt when they did. He lip-synched the words to the hymns. He noticed that a few people (including the man he was tailing) did not go forward to receive communion, so he stayed seated.

Ernest Hemingway defined courage as grace under pressure. I don't know much about courage—it seems too fine a word to be used in detective work. But I can't think of a better description for the way the investigator handled that situation—grace under pressure.

Having good social skills doesn't preclude you from being rude; they just allow you to choose the occasion. There is nothing to gain by being rude out of ignorance.

THE EMOTIONAL QUALITIES

The emotional demands of the detective's craft can be divided into two categories: those that are a function of the job, and those that are a result of the job. The former are occupational demands; the latter are personal.

Occupational Demands

Detective work is odd. Almost every important decision you make is based on information you know to be incomplete. And those decisions have to be made with the knowledge that your course of action is limited. Such odd work requires an equally odd assortment of emotional qualities. In order to remain effective, a detective needs:

- Professional distance
- Persistence
- A high tolerance for stress
- A strong sense of self

Professional Distance. I learned about professional distance as a medic in the service. I was only nineteen years old and suddenly in a position in which I had to make life-and-death decisions. The only way I could do the job well was to detach myself emotionally from what was going on. When in a crisis situation, I pretended to be calm and in control. And people believed it. Then a strange thing would happen; the other people would calm down. And then an even stranger thing happened; I actually became calm and in control.

The same lesson applies to detectives, or anybody else. You cannot be effective when you're scared, or disgusted, or angry, or even elated. Any powerful emotion weakens your objectivity and clouds your judgment.

Persistence. It's easy to give up. There are times when the desire to throw up your hands in despair is almost irresistible.

I was trying to locate a witness in a felony case. The witness, however, did not want to be found. He had abandoned his apartment and quit his job. I spoke to his neighbors, his former coworkers, his friends, his landlord. Nobody seemed to know where he was. But on his rental agreement and his employment application, the man had listed his grandmother as his next of kin.

So I locked onto the grandmother. I staked out her

house, hoping he'd show up. I tailed her everywhere she went. I went through her trash for her old telephone bills and called all the numbers. I got the description of the witness's car from the Department of Motor Vehicles in case he drove by her house.

It paid off. It took a while, but one Sunday afternoon he showed up at his grandmother's house. I waited until he finished his visit, then approached him.

As I said, it's easy to give up. Surrender is seductive. When you're facing a brick wall, you have three choices. You can walk away—a reasonable response. You can try to sneak around or over it (my favorite). Or you can just pound your head against it until you break through.

On the other hand, you need to know when persistence slips over the line into obstinacy. You should persist as long as there is a reasonable chance of success, and then just a little longer. Then give it up.

High Stress Tolerance. One of the vexations of detective work is that you alternate between periods of boredom and moments of near panic. You're often involved in situations where you don't fully understand what's happening and have little control over the events taking place. You have to make vitally important decisions based on woefully insufficient information. This is stressful, to say the least.

Stress, frustration, ambiguity, and boredom: these are the detective's version of the four horsemen of the Apocalypse. If you can't deal with them, go work in a hardware store.

Each detective handles stress differently. Some meditate, some take up hobbies, some drink too much. I can't tell you what is best. I haven't decided for myself yet.

Sense of Self. We all want people to like us, to appreciate us, to think well of us. Detectives are no different.
But sometimes detectives have to behave in ways that
don't represent who they really are.

There are times when you have to look stupid or bum-
bling. Or accept insults you ordinarily wouldn't. Or
allow others to see you in an unflattering light. In order
to do that, you need a strong sense of who you really are
down at the bone.

During a strike at a local factory, I was asked to interview some replacement workers who had witnessed an
assault. One of the strikers had been badly beaten by a
pair of strike-breakers. The witnesses agreed to talk to
me, but only at the plant. That meant I had to cross the
picket line. I'd never crossed a picket line in my life.

I supported the strike. I was working for one of the
strikers. I even had friends who worked at the plant and
had walked the picket line. But when I got to the plant,
I couldn't stop at the line to explain why I was crossing
it. If I was seen visiting with the strikers it might have
alienated the people I was going to interview.

So I drove slowly through the crowd of strikers gath-
ered at the gate of the plant. They shouted obscenities at
me and called me a scab. They spit on my car. I felt like
the lowest of the low. I knew I was doing the right thing,
but there was little comfort in the knowledge.

A good detective has to appreciate and respect himself,
and can't depend on anybody else to feel the same way.

Personal Demands

Dashiell Hammett wrote a short story in which he
describes an aging detective: ". . . his gentle eyes behind
gold spectacles and his mild smile, hiding the fact that

fifty years of sleuthing had left him without any feelings at all on any subject."

Hammett had been a detective. He understood that the greatest risk faced by the detective is the risk of becoming emotionally sterile. It isn't the danger of getting beat up or shot, it's the danger of losing emotional balance. Detectives are forced (or allowed) to look into the darker aspects of human nature. They often see an intensity of emotion that forces them to respond by becoming colder and more distant. They see much that is pathetic, corrupt, and ugly. Sometimes they see too much.

Since the job tends to be solitary, it allows time for introspection and reflection on what you've seen. There is danger of becoming hard and cynical; there is danger in *not* becoming hard and cynical. And even more perilous is the willing abandonment of compassion and humanity.

Near my office was a small store where I would stop two or three times a week to buy a snack and a soft drink. The store was owned by a cantankerous old woman who kept a couple of cats and an ancient, arthritic dog. After a few months she saw that I liked her animals and she became a little less crabby. We never became friends, but we grew accustomed to each other. Eventually we began to talk to each other and I discovered she was just peevish because she was old and tired.

One winter day, I went to the store and found it surrounded by police cruisers. The old woman had been robbed and murdered. She and her dog had been stabbed to death. A few days later, I was assigned to help in the defense of the person accused of killing her.

One of my duties was to photograph the scene. I'd become accustomed to gore as a medic, so the dried blood on the floor and spattered on the walls wasn't disturbing in itself. As I immersed myself in the technical aspects of shooting the photographs, I forgot who the blood belonged to. In order to shoot one particular spatter pattern, I had to stand in a corner where the blood had pooled. Blood, when it dries, becomes flaky, and it crunched under my sneakers.

I finished the job and began to walk back to my office. For some reason I turned and looked back toward the store. I saw I was leaving a trail of faint copper-colored footprints in the snow behind me. I checked the bottom of my sneakers. Some of the crusted blood had stuck in the grooves.

For a moment I was paralyzed with horror, and I felt like screaming. But only for a moment. Habit and training took over. I swished my shoes in a puddle of melting snow, calming myself as the blood speckled the puddle. Then I walked back to my office.

It's tough to find a healthy balance between compassion and emotional self-defense. But you must. If you don't, you may wind up an emotional eunuch like Hammett's detective. Or curled up in a ball in your closet, silently screaming.

THE PHYSICAL QUALITIES

This is the least important attribute of the detective. You don't need to be strong, you don't need to be nimble, you don't need to be in perfect physical condition. Those things can be helpful, but they're not critical.

Still, you ought to be in reasonably good shape. You won't have to run a marathon, but you may have to tail a fast walker. You won't have to bench press twice your body weight, but you may have to move some heavy boxes. You won't have to scale cliffs, but you may have to climb several flights of stairs without puffing and panting.

What *is* critical is stamina. A good detective needs the ability and, more important, the willingness to endure.

Not just to persist in the face of long hours, solitude, and stress, but to endure physical discomfort as well: The aching feet and knees after hours of standing and walking, the back and eye strain from long hours spent hunched over countless ledgers in some poorly lit office, the upset stomach from too many indigestible meals eaten on the run.

Television detectives suffer, and shrug off, bullet wounds and concussions. Real detectives have more mundane afflictions—hemorrhoids, bad digestion, and tension headaches.

Not very romantic, is it?

I hope by now you have some idea of what it takes to be a good detective. I also hope you will examine yourself carefully, that you will give yourself the same cold and objective scrutiny you'd give to a case, to see if you have what it takes. Because the last thing the world needs is another bad investigator.

In later chapters I'll suggest investigative techniques you might want to try. There are a lot of reasons *not* to try them. You might make a mistake and look foolish; somebody might get upset with you; you could waste a lot of time.

Those are good reasons. I doubt I'd use them, if I wasn't getting paid. But you must, you absolutely *must*, be willing to look foolish, to waste time, to risk the anger of others when the circumstances demand it.

That's all it takes—nothing really out of the ordinary, just ordinary things in extraordinary combinations and a willingness to put your client's needs before your own.

You can do it. The question you have to ask yourself is this: Do you really want to?

When we were working in Key West one week, Greg taught me how to tail. I recommend the Keys for the beginning detective. Everybody wears dark glasses and brightly colored clothes, and everybody is looking at everybody else.

There are lots of bars in Key West, and all of them seem to have mirrors. Mirrors, as you'll learn, are a detective's dream. Sadly, I discovered that the caution I take when practicing law—checking and double checking every step—got in my way when I tried to practice tailing. Too much can happen while you're being careful.

I learned how to tail on the flat ground of Florida. About a year later, I was trying to tail a guy in San Francisco, where the entire town is built on hills and the sidewalks have stairs. I discovered three things about tailing in San Francisco: (1) I have a tendency to watch my feet when going down stairs; (2) you can't watch your subject and your feet at the same time; and (3) if you try to watch your subject and your feet at the same time, you'll fall down.

R.G.

Chapter 2

THE GENTLE ART OF TAILING

I n this chapter you will learn how to perform a solo tail, both on foot and by car. You will learn how to blend in with a crowd, to alter your appearance, to identify your subject from a distance. You'll learn the significance of details and how to use shield cars. This is the true stuff.

Tailing is the quintessence of the detective's craft, the distillate of all the detective's skills blended into a strange, complex, and heady drink. It's often frustrating, sometimes tiring, and occasionally frightening. But when it works, it's intoxicating.

Tailing requires a feel for the behavior of the individual and the crowd. You have to be in tune with the person you're tailing and with the people around you. You have to balance risk against caution, confidence against cockiness, anxiety against need. You must be patient; you must be alert; you must be intuitive, clever, and persistent. Above all, you must be invisible. You must be like a mist in comfortable shoes.

As with most detective work, there are no solid rules to tailing. Well, there is one—don't get caught. Being spotted by your subject (detectives usually say "getting made" or "burned") is more than a failure of technique. It can be fatal to the investigation.

Tailing is a reactive skill. Your subject acts; you react. You can try to anticipate his behavior, even predict it.

But it's an egregious mistake to rely on that prediction. If you feel the need to prove how clever you are (and most of us do occasionally), make mental bets with yourself about what your subject will do. But never put the job at risk.

Generally, tailing falls into two categories:

- On foot
- By car

Though these are the most common categories, you're not restricted to them. People have been followed by aircraft and by boat. (A remarkable number of philanderers want to make love on the high seas.) Detectives have used bicycles, golf carts, you name it. I know a detective who tailed his subject while jogging in the park. Anywhere people go, there is a detective willing to follow.

Ideally, a tail is performed by a team of operatives in frequent communication by radio. However, such a production is often prohibitively expensive, and most often the detective must conduct a solo tail.

Even working solo, you begin with a singular advantage: very few people expect to be followed. It's mainly in movies that the subject of a tail keeps looking over his shoulder to see if he's being followed. Even so, some people are more suspicious than others. Women having affairs tend to be more cautious than men, but even errant wives find it difficult to believe that another person would actually follow them everywhere they go.*

Offsetting this advantage is a random universe. People are unpredictable. Events unfold in unforeseeable ways. The detective is at the mercy of the subject's whims and

---

* There is an exception to this—women who have been stalked by a former lover or spouse. These women, understandably, are often very much aware of the men around them.

vagaries. Seemingly rational people will come to a tire-screeching halt at a yard sale, leaving you to go sailing by, desperately looking for an inconspicuous place to pull over. Or you'll stub your toe on an uneven sidewalk and your subject will disappear while you hop up and down on one foot and mutter useless curses. On one occasion, I lost a subject when I was stopped by a police officer and lectured for jaywalking. It was probably the only time in the history of that city that a person was actually stopped for jaywalking.

ON FOOT

This is the way most people picture a detective—shadowing some shady character down into the city's bowels. They conjure up an image of a lone man in a trenchcoat leaning against a street lamp, pretending to read a newspaper.

It's not like that. You can dress like Sam Spade if you want, lean against any number of lamp posts, and enjoy your image of yourself. Or you can do the job. Conducting a solo tail on foot is a difficult and sensitive task. But with a little preparation, patience, and practice, you can do it.

Preparation

The key to conducting a solo tail is preparation. The motto "be prepared" is one thing—probably the *only* thing—detectives have in common with Boy Scouts.

Study your subject. If possible, interview someone who knows the subject well. Try to examine recent photographs. Look for gross features that are unlikely to change, such as:

- the shape of the head
- the slope of the shoulders
- the length of the legs

Disregard such small features as eye color or ear shape; if you're close enough to your subject to determine his eye color, you're too close. Besides, the subject is rarely facing you. That's why they call it tailing.

There are a lot of details to note during the initial phases of the tail. For example:

- *The subject's walk.* Most people have a distinctive walk, a bounce in their step or a tendency to drag their heels. You'll find people tend to grow into their walk—the younger the subject, the less distinctive the walk.
- *The subject's posture.* Posture can be equally characteristic. Many people can be easily identified by the way they carry themselves. A good slouch or hypercorrect posture is a gift to a detective. I once tailed a retired Marine Corps sergeant; I could have followed him in the dark just by listening for the sharp heel strikes of his military stride.
- *The subject's clothing.* Pay attention to the subject's clothing, but don't use it as your primary means of identification. Clothing, although often distinct, is unreliable. If a person suspects he is be being followed, his clothing is usually the first thing he'll change. But even people who go to the effort of changing their clothes usually neglect to wear different shoes and almost never switch their watch.
- *Idiosyncratic gestures.* Again, many people have distinct idiosyncratic gestures. For example, a male subject may have a nervous habit of straightening his tie. A long-haired subject may frequently give a distinctive flick of the head to clear the hair from his face.

Becoming familiar with such distinguishing physical and habitual characteristics is not as difficult as it sounds. You can probably identify your friends and family from a distance that would render their facial features a blur. Baseball fans can often tell players apart by the way they swing the bat. All it requires is that you exercise your powers of observation.

Tactics

Unless you are using electronic location devices (which will be discussed later in the chapter on technology), you have to keep your subject in sight. However, this doesn't mean you need to keep constant direct visual contact with your subject. In fact, staring at the subject will likely draw his attention. Many detectives are slightly superstitious. Some primitive instinct makes us think a subject can "feel" us if we watch too closely.

So a good detective rarely looks directly at the subject being followed, choosing instead to rely on such aids as:

- *Reflections.* Fortunately for detectives the city is full of reflective surfaces—car and shop windows, for example, or those plexiglass bus shelters, even puddles. Use them.
- *Peripheral vision.* When there are no reflective surfaces, use your peripheral vision. You can determine the width of your peripheral vision by holding your arms directly out in front of you with a pencil in each hand. Look straight ahead at a fixed spot and slowly move your arms apart until you can no longer see the pencils. You can (and should) practice using your peripheral vision. A simple exercise you can do at any time is to stare straight ahead at a fixed point and note the objects you can see out of the corners

of your eyes. People process a lot more visual information than they realize. Our brains selectively eliminate most of the visual information they receive because it's irrelevant. With just a little practice, howecer, you can literally widen your horizons.

- *"Placing" the subject.* Visually "placing" your subject is a critical tailing technique. *Placing* simply means noting the subject's direction in relation to yours and estimating his speed of travel and the direction in which he is moving. It allows you to maintain contact with the subject without having to focus all of your attention on him. That way you can avoid tripping on the sidewalk or colliding with other pedestrians.

The two most critical elements in maintaining contact with the subject are *distance* and *direction*.

Proper tailing distance depends entirely on the circumstance. You need to be close enough to identify the subject and to be able to react to unexpected moves on his part. But you also need to remain far enough away so that you don't attract his attention. In a crowd you can—in fact, you must—follow a little more closely. On nearly deserted streets, allow the subject more distance, even at the risk of losing him. It's better to break off the tail than to get "made" and alert the subject. Good detectives know when to invoke the Scarlett O'Hara rule: Tomorrow is another day.

Direction, in this context, means where the subject is compared to where you are. A solo tail is almost always conducted from behind the subject (there are rare exceptions, as will be noted), but this doesn't mean you're locked onto the same side of the street. Tailing a subject from the opposite side of the street decreases the risk of being spotted. As you might guess, every advantage carries its own risk. Your line of sight can be blocked by traffic or parked vehicles; the use of reflective surfaces becomes riskier; crossing the street in a hurry can attract attention, and put you in danger from traffic.

I know a detective who, on a long-term solo tail, actually followed his subject from the front. He bought a cyclist's mirror (an inexpensive mirror the size of a quarter designed to attach to cycling helmets and caps by an alligator clip) and attached it to the visor of his baseball cap. Although the limited viewing surface of the mirror made it tricky, he was able to keep an eye on the subject behind him. I wouldn't recommend this as a standard technique, but it could be useful under the proper circumstances.

Clothing

A long-term tail always increases the odds of getting "made." To reduce those odds, the detective needs to be as nondescript as possible. This fact is often overlooked by Hollywood. The television detective's carefully styled hair and flashy clothes would condemn a real detective, even assuming he could afford the wardrobe.

Again, there are no firm rules, but here are a few general guidelines:

1. *Avoid bright colors.* They attract attention.
2. *Wear comfortable shoes.* This is critical. Assume you'll be on your feet for a long time. Many shoe companies now market walking shoes, some with gel or air in the soles. These innovations have brought smiles to the faces of sore-footed detectives.
3. *Wear nothing new; it attracts attention.* For the same reason, wear nothing with writing on it. Wear nothing highly starched; it quickly becomes uncomfortable.

4. *Except when limited by circumstance, choose clothing in which you feel at ease.* The more comfortable you are, the less likely it is that you'll look out of place. A good detective is as comfortable in a tuxedo as a fatigue jacket. People tend to notice a person who is uncomfortable in their clothes. I know a man who, like a lot of private investigators, is a former police officer. He's a good man and a good detective, but he's worthless on a tail. The moment people see him, they think, *That man is a cop.* He looks like a cop because he wears his clothes like a cop. Regardless of what he wears, he wears it like a uniform.

5. *Dress for your audience.* For example, you shouldn't wear a Hawaiian shirt while tailing a subject in the financial district. Nor should you wear a white shirt and tie when on the boardwalk at the beach.

The primary consideration in choosing your clothes should be the job. Your personal feelings about your appearance, your individual sense of style, and your comfort and ego should all be subordinate to the job.

Once, to blend in at the power-lunch restaurants and fern bars frequented by the subject I was following, I wore a suit and tie every day for a week. I am not fond of a tie. At the end of that week, the subject decided to stop at a bar where I occasionally drink. I gave him a couple of minutes to get settled, then eased into the bar. As I walked in, a friend noticed me. He stared slack-jawed at me for a moment, then stood and pointed me out to his companions. "Look," he said. "It's himself, in a tie." Then he demanded, in a loud drunken voice, to know if I'd been out looking for honest work.

I had to abandon the tail for a few days.

There are times when a detective needs to subtly alter his appearance. The key here is subtlety. Don't try to be a master of disguise. Leave your false whiskers and wig at home along with your trench coat. The idea is to camouflage yourself, to blend into the background. A few carefully chosen items of clothing and accessories will usually suffice. Here are some suggestions:

- *Layer your clothing.* Remove and add items sporadically and in different combinations.
- *Glasses.* Alternate between regular glasses and sunglasses. If you don't wear corrective lenses, you can often buy frames with clear lenses from better optical stores.
- *Hats.* Bring a well-worn baseball cap, one of an unobtrusive color, without clever sayings. Alternate between wearing it and carrying it. It is unlikely you'll be seen holding it—even in a small crowd people rarely see anything below the shoulders. A beret is compact and can be shoved in the detective's pocket or handbag. Of course, although a detective in New York City might be able to wear a beret and not attract attention, a detective in Moline, Illinois, would have a hard time carrying it off.
- *Hair.* Women can make startling changes in their appearance simply by undoing a bun (not everything you see in the movies is nonsense).

Occasionally, regardless of how good you are or what precautions you take, you'll find yourself face to face with your subject. Not because you have been burned, but because people are unpredictable. Perhaps the subject entered a crowded elevator and you were forced to follow in order to see where he got off. Maybe he was lost in thought, walked past his destination, and suddenly turned around to go back.

When this happens, don't panic. Do something rude. Scratch your crotch or pick your nose, something offensive. When confronted with such behavior, people generally look away. Or at least they avoid looking you in the face. You may lose a little dignity, but dignity is a commodity the working detective cannot afford.

As with every other aspect of detective work, the key is to pay attention. I once tailed a photographer who walked with a pronounced slump in his left shoulder, the result, I assume, of constantly carrying a heavy camera bag. The slump allowed me to follow him from half a block away from the opposite side of the street. One evening he led me to a notorious gay bar.

I hesitated before following him in. I tried to tell myself I was hesitating because I was afraid of getting burned. I wasn't concerned he'd recognize me from the street, but that if he saw my face in the bar he might then notice me later on the street. People in pick-up bars tend to look at the faces of the other customers.

But the real reason I hesitated was I was afraid. I'd never been in a gay bar. What if somebody I knew saw me going in? What if somebody I knew was already inside?

After a three-minute debate with myself, professionalism won; I had to go in. I was getting paid, after all, to see what this fellow was up to. Besides, it seemed silly to worry about the appearance of entering a gay bar. A bar is a bar, I told myself. Spending time in bars is part of the job. How different could a gay bar be?

The answer is, not that different. Aside from the music, which was right out of the forties, and the fact that men (some of whom were in drag) were dancing with other men, it was pretty much like any other bar. In one regard, though, the bar was a detective's dream— there were mirrors everywhere.

I sat on a bar stool near the door, ordered a beer, and searched the mirrors. But I couldn't spot my photographer. He wasn't sitting at the bar, nor could I see him on the dance floor or at one of the tables.

I'd just about worked up the courage to look for him in one of the rest rooms (should I choose Guys or Dolls?) when I was approached by a man in drag who asked me to dance. I considered it, thinking it would allow me to look for my man without being too conspicuous. (How conspicuous can you be dancing with a man in drag?) But I declined. I didn't want to lose my seat by the door in case my photographer left.

In the mirror, I watched the man in drag turn away to ask somebody else. He had a distinct slump in his left shoulder.

Gender identity may come and go, but posture is forever.

By Car

There used to be a television show in which the protagonist—a private detective operating in Hawaii—often conducted a tail while driving a Ferrari. A bright red Ferrari. It must have stood out like a clown's nose in the subject's rearview mirror. Despite this obvious handicap, the detective managed to tail his subject all over the island of Oahu. Ferraris must be as common as coconuts in Hawaii, because he never got made.

I have to admit it. I'm not that good.

A solo tail in a car is difficult under the best conditions. But to burden yourself with a Ferrari is absurd. It's worse than absurd; it's unprofessional.

A detective should consider the following qualities when selecting a vehicle for tailing:

- *Appearance:* Obviously, the vehicle should be inconspicuous. Clean without being too shiny; of a common color (blue is the most common, followed by green); free of bumper stickers. And no vanity tags, please. I knew an investigator whose tags spelled SNOOP. They should have spelled STUPID.
- *Performance:* The vehicle should be in good working condition. It should run quietly, without emitting a lot of exhaust fumes or clouds of burning oil. Power is handy; it's not always needed, but on those rare occasions when you tail, say, a subject in a bright red Ferrari, you'll want it.
- *Comfort:* This is a quality too often overlooked. Detectives spend an inordinate amount of time in their cars. Reclining seats are almost mandatory.

At a party, where I'd made a few disparaging remarks about detectives in bright red Ferraris, I was asked what sort of car was best suited for tailing. The answer is easy. A rental car.

Rental cars are wonderful. They come in a variety of colors and sizes and are easily changed, like a steel wardrobe. Just remember to peel off the rental agency decals; they're one more detail that might draw attention.

Preparation

As with tailing on foot, preparation is vital. Plan ahead. Visit the site where you'll begin the tail. If possible, determine the direction the subject is likely to start in and park your car accordingly. A lot of the stress involved in a solo tail can be alleviated with a few minutes forethought.

Before beginning the tail, make certain you have the following:

1. *Full tank of gas.* This detail is so obvious that it sometimes is forgotten.
2. *Maps.* Get good ones; they're worth the money.
3. *Sunglasses, preferably polarized.* It would be stupid to lose your subject because you're squinting into the glare of the sun.
4. *Change.* Lots of it—for tolls, snacks, and drinks.

Plan the excursion as you would a lengthy trip, even if you think you'll only be in the car for thirty minutes.

Familiarize yourself with the car you'll be following. You should, of course, note the make, model, color, year, and license number. But don't stop there. Also check for

- Dents and other blemishes
- Bumper stickers
- Antenna arrangement
- Tire tread design (which can be very important when tailing in the country)
- Taillight design, for tailing at night

Always try to learn more than you think you'll need to know. And don't be surprised when that's not enough.

One winter a woman hired me to follow her husband, whom she suspected of having an affair. She wanted me to find out where he was going after work. I got as much information as I could from her, including the fact that her husband drove a company truck to and from the plant where he was employed. Although she didn't know the make, model, year, or license number, her description of the vehicle was such that I wasn't worried about missing it. It was a late model pick-up truck (pick-ups are great—they sit high off the ground, making them easier to spot in traffic) with a company logo on the door. Best of all, she said the truck was painted bright orange.

At a quarter to five the next afternoon, I was parked near the entrance to the plant, waiting for the husband to leave. Shortly after five o'clock, as the early winter dusk set in, a bright orange pick-up with a company logo came out of the gate. It was so bright it looked radioactive. I grinned to myself as I waited for a few "shield" cars to insert themselves between us. But I didn't grin long. As I started to ease into place, another orange pick-up drove out of the plant. And then another. And still another. Seventeen bright orange trucks in total, all with company logos on the door. I just sat there, feeling like a fool, watching the parade of orange trucks.

That night, shortly after midnight, I drove to the client's home. Sitting in the drive was her husband's bright orange pick-up. I parked half a block away, took out a small tack hammer from the trunk, walked quietly back to her house, and smashed the truck's left taillight.

The next afternoon, when the legion of bright orange trucks emerged, only one had a shattered left taillight. The rest was easy.

Well, as easy as it ever gets.

Tactics

There is one major advantage to tailing by car over tailing by foot. A car is confining. Your subject can't suddenly decide to step into a doorway, or walk down the up escalator. Everywhere your subject goes, he has to take a ton of steel with him. Cars are unwieldy. They limit where your subject can go. Traffic laws can also work in your favor. Fortunately, most people obey most of the rules of the road. A detective conducting a solo tail dreads the thought of an illegal U-turn.

Unfortunately, those same limitations also apply to you. In a car you're unable to respond as quickly or as subtly as on foot. Nor can you violate traffic laws without risking notice—of either the subject or the police. The same laws that prevent your subject from making U-turns allow him to turn right on a red light, leaving you to pound your steering wheel in frustration.

There are two related elements that demand constant attention while engaged in a solo tail by car.

1. Shield cars
2. Distance

These, in turn, are dependent on external conditions, such as:

• Traffic density
• Traffic speed and flow
• Weather
• Lighting conditions

You have limited control over the first two elements, shield cars and distance. You have no control over the rest. Once again it's you versus a random universe.

Shield cars are vehicles you allow between your car and your subject's car. The number of shield cars depends on external conditions and your self-confidence. For example, you can allow more shield cars on an interstate highway, where exits are limited and fewer surprises can happen. Conversely, in dense city traffic you'll want fewer shield cars (perhaps only one or two) between yourself and your subject.

Too many shield cars makes it extremely difficult to maintain visual contact with your subject and increases the odds of losing him. Too few shield cars increases the odds of getting burned.

Distance is more of a factor when there are few or no shield cars, such as in the country or in the city during the early morning hours. Maintaining appropriate distance works much the same way as determining the proper number of shield cars. During bad weather and at night, tighten up the distance between yourself and your subject.

Oddly enough, people who drive too fast are usually easier to follow than those who drive too slow. Speeders are paying attention to the road, looking for openings in traffic and watching for cops. Loafers, on the other hand, disrupt traffic and spend a lot of time glancing fearfully in the rearview mirror.

The toughest tail I ever conducted was of an old woman, the grandmother I mentioned in Chapter 1. As I said, I wasn't interested in her but in her grandson, with whom she was very close. I was watching her in the hope that she'd lead me to him.

The woman drove everywhere; six blocks to the market, eight blocks to the post office. And she rarely drove faster than twenty-five miles per hour. That wouldn't have been a problem except that most of the streets in her neighborhood had four lanes—two in each direction—and the speed limit was forty-five. One car driving twenty-five in a forty-five zone stands out; two cars looks like a small funeral. It couldn't be done subtly. Eventually, I switched to a bicycle and followed her from the sidewalks.

It worked, by the way. I found the kid.

Summary

At first tailing can seem intimidating. There is so much that is beyond your control, so much that can go wrong. The first time I conducted a solo tail, I was a nervous wreck. I lost the subject within a few blocks. *How can anybody ever do this?* I wondered.

Well, you do it like this:

1. *Prepare.* Learn as much as you possibly can, but accept the fact that it may not be enough.
2. *Plan ahead.* From the beginning, control all the factors you can. Give some thought to those you can't control, but don't focus too much on them.
3. *Pay attention.* Be aware of what is taking place around you, but don't get bogged down in meaningless details.
4. *Relax.* When you get too anxious, you make mistakes.
5. *Know when to quit.* Perseverance is good; stubbornness is not. Don't blow a tail because you're too tired or irritated to do a good job.

Tailing is perhaps the toughest skill a detective has to learn. Often, it's the most rewarding. It's certainly the most fun. And, with practice and patience, you can do it.

But *if* you do it, *if* you choose to tail somebody, make certain you have a good reason. This is not something you do for your own amusement. There are laws against harassment (see Chapter 10). If you make the decision to conduct a tail, then do it right. Do it in a professional manner. The job comes first, always—not your temper, not your comfort, not your ego. The job.

As much as I love my work, there are times when I don't want to be a lawyer. I want to be something else. When that happens, I talk Greg into letting me go out on an investigation with him. I usually learn something new, and the experience always makes me appreciate my own job more.

On one such occasion, I convinced Greg to let me serve a subpoena. It was for a woman who, for nearly two years, had listened to the man in the next apartment beat his wife. One day, after the man left the apartment, the wife set their bed on fire. Unfortunately, a good part of the apartment building burned along with the bed. The wife was charged with arson.

The woman was needed to testify about the battering in court. We went to the woman's new apartment and, while Greg waited in the car, I knocked on the door. She answered and I explained that I had a subpoena for her. I hadn't even finished talking when she slammed the door in my face. After recovering from the shock, I knocked on the door again. But she refused to answer.

I was angry. How dare that woman shut the door in my face. I wanted to serve that subpoena more than anything. So, very early the next morning, Greg and I staked out the apartment house. We were waiting for the woman to come out and go to work. As she left the apartment building, we'd nail her with the subpoena. I had to be there, because I was the only person who would recognize her. I was jazzed. My first stakeout.

But we just sat there. And sat there. And sat there. Greg sort of slumped down and became part of the car seat. But I was going nuts. Where was she? What was she doing? What if she decided not to go to work that day? What if I missed her? Why wasn't Greg as nervous as I was? He just sat there, like nothing was going on. Bastard. Where in the hell was she?

I swear we waited for nearly two hours before the woman finally came out. Greg says it was closer to forty minutes.

Maybe I've got the wrong attitude.

R.G.

Chapter 3

WATCHING AND WAITING
the quiet craft of surveillance

Stakeout. The word has sort of a gritty, sexy ring to it, doesn't it? Maybe that's why private detectives don't use it. We know better.

We usually refer to it as "surveillance." The term is gritty enough, but not very alluring. And that's a pretty accurate description of the job: lots of grit, not much allure.

Essentially, surveillance is the craft of seeing without being seen. At its worst, and it is usually at its worst, it can be mind-numbingly dull. At its best, surveillance can be oddly exciting—not thrilling, but stimulating in a warped, quiet way.

Surveillance is often done in conjunction with tailing. You need to scrutinize the activities of a certain person, so you follow and watch them. Tailing and surveillance go together like chicken fried steak and cream gravy.

In some cases, however, you are more interested in a place than a person. For example, you may want to identify the people who enter a certain office or apartment. On other occasions the place may be simply a link to the person you're interested in. Once, while trying to locate a man who was avoiding a subpoena, I set up a surveillance on his lover and waited for him to show up. It only took about three hours.

There are two aspects to surveillance: external and internal. The external aspect of surveillance has to do with the active techniques, the methods for "casing" a location, the use of alternate spotting locations, the act of observation itself. The internal aspect has to do with the way the detective works the surveillance mentally, the way he prepares himself and deals with the demand that he be tirelessly observant. This aspect is normally the most difficult for the detective, beginners and old hands alike.

For example, I was assisting another investigator in a surveillance and tail. I'd never worked with this man before, but he had several years more field experience than I did, and I knew his reputation. I was looking forward to learning from the experience.

The subject was a man who was having an affair with one of the client's daughters. The client felt the man was a playboy and a scoundrel; he wasn't pleased with the thought of such a man being involved with his "baby girl." He believed the man was sleeping with other women as well, and he'd hired the investigator to confirm his suspicions.

On the first evening of the assignment, we met near the subject's office at four o'clock in the afternoon. My partner parked his car in a place where he could see both the subject's office and his car. I took a position across the street in the parking lot of a small shopping mall. We had two-way radios but, after making a radio check to ensure they were functioning properly, we decided not to use them until the subject was moving. People tend to notice men in cars speaking into walkie-talkies. The last thing either of us wanted was to attract attention.

Since my role was secondary—I wouldn't be needed until the subject began to move—I didn't settle into my normal surveillance mode. Instead, I listened to the car radio and thumbed through a magazine. By five-thirty, I was beginning to get impatient. By six o'clock, I was cursing the subject for working so late. I hate an over-achiever. By six-thirty, I began to wonder if my partner had let the subject slip. I decided to break radio silence and find out what, if anything, was going on. So I clicked the radio a few times. There was no response from my partner. I broke radio silence and asked him for a status report. Still nothing.

I sat there for a moment, thinking of all the things that could have gone wrong. My radio could have malfunctioned. Or *his* radio could have malfunctioned. Who knows, maybe there was heavy sunspot activity that interfered with the radio transmission.

In the end, I decided it didn't matter *why* he hadn't responded. All that mattered was that he hadn't. I figured my partner had probably signaled me and I hadn't heard. I immediately became convinced that while I was listening to the radio and catching up on the news of the day, the subject had driven off with my poor partner in pursuit, wondering what the hell had happened to me.

Before giving the surveillance up entirely, I decided to make a quick check of the office parking lot. I got out of my car and walked across the street to see what I could learn. There, in the otherwise empty parking lot, was the other investigator's car. He was slumped over in it, sound asleep, and snoring. It sounded like *The Texas Chain Saw Massacre*.

I didn't wake him. I just stuck a note under his windshield wiper: Get a job.

In surveillance, the internal and external aspects must work in coordination. They are absolutely dependent on each other. Being well prepared or being in the right spot is of no help if you're napping while the action takes place.

EXTERNAL ASPECTS

There are only three components to surveillance: preparation, the surveillance itself, and breaking off. Remember, the whole point is to see without being seen. If you prepare properly, work it properly, and break off properly, your subject will never know you were there.

Preparation

As with all facets of detective work, preparation is the first consideration. Since surveillance is usually done in conjunction with tailing, many of the same preparatory steps are required. In addition, take the following steps:

1. Case the site.
2. Dress appropriately.
3. Be well rested.
4. Have the proper equipment.
5. Bring a snack.

These are common sense steps. I mention them because it's amazing how frequently people fail to use their common sense.

Case the site. This isn't always possible. There will be times when you tail somebody to an unfamiliar location and have to set up an impromptu surveillance. When that happens, all you can do is improvise.

But if you can case the site, do it. Visit the site at a quiet hour. Locate all the exits. Identify alternative spotting locations and consider how quickly you can shift between them without breaking surveillance. Pay attention to details—street lamps, traffic conditions, and the like.

Dress appropriately. If possible, wear clothing that fits the circumstances. (See the section on clothing in the previous chapter.)

You want to be comfortable as well as inconspicuous. Most surveillances are conducted from a car. While that offers some protection from the elements, it doesn't help much during extremely hot or cold weather. The only thing more miserable than sweltering in a car on an airless summer day is freezing in that same car in the middle of January. You're supposed to be inconspicuous, remember? So you can't run your car's heater or air conditioner. A running car might attract attention. This is especially true in the winter, when the exhaust is so visible.

The worst surveillance I ever conducted took place during the winter in New England. Winter in New England can be savage. I had to be at the site at 5:00 A.M., which may be the most dismal hour on the clock. I wore long underwear, two pairs of wool socks, a flannel shirt, and a bulky sweater, all under a snowmobile suit. I was so cumbersome in that outfit that I could barely bend my leg enough to engage the clutch. It was just barely enough to keep me warm, though. It was just about perfect, in other words. If I was any warmer, I'd probably have fallen asleep. Any colder, and I'd probably be missing a few fingers and toes now.

Be well rested. Try to get plenty of sleep before beginning the surveillance. Or bring along something to compensate for it. You may need to be awake and alert for a very long time. NoDoz and related products can help you extend your effective hours, although you pay for it later. Coffee is a short-term remedy for weariness, but caffeine also stimulates the need to urinate, which can be a major problem.

Have the proper equipment. Binoculars, a spotting scope, or night-vision devices are often useful during surveillance. Sound amplification devices, like the small dish antennas you see on the sidelines of football games, can be extremely handy. And if you're going to be taking photographs, make sure you have the proper lenses and film of the appropriate speed. Ensure that the batteries for any electronic equipment are working and that you have spare batteries just in case. This isn't rocket science, but equipment failure at the wrong time could be disastrous. We'll discuss investigative equipment in Chapter 11.

Bring a snack. Food is important. You don't burn a lot of calories while conducting a surveillance, but you need to keep hunger at bay in order to rid yourself of the distraction.

Trail mix is the ideal snoop snack. It's a conglomeration of nuts, raisins, M&Ms, granola, and just about anything else that won't melt. It's a good source of quick energy and doesn't spoil.

For a drink, a little tea or coffee is good. The key phrase, though, is *a little.* Too much fluid can lead to calamity. A thermos of ice chips works well in the summer. Ice chips keep you from getting too thirsty without filling you with fluid.

I make these recommendations based on experience. One of my first cases as a detective involved the surveillance of a doctor's office. My client wanted to know if a certain person was seeing the doctor. The reasons for his curiosity aren't relevant now; all you need to know is that I was hired to watch a specific office for a specific person on a specific day.

I hadn't conducted a prolonged surveillance before, but I'd discussed it with other detectives and thought I could handle the situation. The evening before the actual surveillance, I drove to the doctor's office, parked nearby, and made a foot reconnaissance of the area. I noticed the office had entrances in the front and on the side. Both entrances were visible from the street. I also located three or four good secondary spotting locations.

The next morning I was at the doctor's office by 7:00 A.M., a full two hours before it opened. I had my choice of parking spaces and chose one where I could see both entrances clearly.

I was both nervous and excited. I was being a real detective, doing real detective stuff. I loved it—for the first hour.

I was totally unprepared for how tedious a surveillance can be. The first hour seemed to flash by. The second hour was a little slower, and the third seemed positively sluggish.

Not knowing how long I'd have to wait for the subject to arrive, I'd brought along enough food and drink for nine or ten hours. I figured the food would help me remain alert. Instead, it was distracting. I kept thinking about it. And even worse, the thought of all that food made me unnaturally hungry. By eleven o'clock, about four hours after I began the surveillance, I'd decided I should eat a little of the food, just so I wouldn't be so distracted by it. By noon I'd consumed all the food and most of the milk and soda.

Around one o'clock, I began to feel the need to relieve myself. This *never* happened to detectives in the movies. I couldn't leave—what if the person I was looking for arrived while I was searching for a rest room? On the other hand, I didn't relish the idea of wetting my pants.

I got out of the car, thinking a little activity would take my mind off my bladder. I spent the next hour coasting between the spotting locations I'd noted the night before. I couldn't stand still. The need was becoming urgent.

By two-thirty my bladder felt like it was the size of a soccer ball. I was certain it would rupture and I'd die of septicemia, if that's what it is you die from when your bladder explodes. Whatever it's called, it's *not* how detectives are supposed to die.

Finally, driven by desperation and unable to think of a better solution, I got back in the car, unfolded an empty milk carton and urinated in it. You have to be both nimble and patient to urinate into a milk carton while sitting in a car on a public street. Nimble, patient, and desperate.

It might have been worth it if the subject had appeared. She never did.

The Surveillance Itself

The actual act of surveillance is simple. You just watch and pay attention. Anybody with decent eyesight, or eyesight correctable by lenses, can do it. All you have to do is observe. It's simple.

The trick, however, is to see without being seen. That's more difficult, but not as hard as it sounds. It just requires a little thought. Here are some things to consider:

1. Surveillance method
2. Spotting locations
3. Concealment

If you pay attention and apply your common sense to these matters, you shouldn't have any problems. We'll examine each item in turn.

Surveillance Methods. There are three basic methods of surveillance:

- From a vehicle
- On foot
- From a building

Most surveillance is done from a parked vehicle. Th.
has a great many advantages. You're protected from the
elements, you're instantly prepared to tail your subject,
any equipment you might need is handy, and the vehicle
provides partial concealment.

On the other hand, vehicles are large and unwieldy,
which limits you mainly to streets and parking lots. And
while you may be protected from rain, sleet, hail, snow,
and wind, you aren't protected from excessive heat in
the summer or extreme cold in the winter. Remember,
you can't use the heater or the air conditioner without
being conspicuous.

Occasionally, a surveillance will be conducted on foot.
This is usually the case when the object of the surveillance is located away from a public road. I know a team
of detectives who followed their subject on a camping
trip. They tailed him in a canoe and camped half a mile
away. When they returned, they were covered with mos-
quito bites and tick-ridden. But they got the evidence
they needed.

Foot surveillance isn't limited to extreme circumstances. On a long surveillance, I often alternate between
vehicle and foot surveillance. It breaks the monotony
and allows me to stretch my cramped muscles.

A foot surveillance has the advantage of allowing
movement. In addition, it tends to keep detectives more
alert and gives them more freedom in selecting spotting
locations. However, a foot surveillance greatly limits the
amount of equipment available to you. A person carrying field glasses on a city street is likely to attract some
attention, even in cities like New York or San Francisco,
where people are used to seeing almost anything. Being
on foot also leaves you ill prepared for a quick exit
should the subject decide to leave suddenly.

On occasion, a surveillance will be conducted from
a building. This could be a public building, such as a

diner, or a private one, such as an empty office or motel room. Generally, this type of surveillance is most useful when you are interested in a specific place rather than a specific person.

For example, during a divorce case, I had to conduct a surveillance on a small, suburban bungalow. My client's husband was a motorcycle enthusiast, and with her financial help, he'd purchased and restored four old motorcycles. However, when discussing the property settlement, he claimed the motorcycles had all been stolen—all four of them. His wife suspected he was storing them in a buddy's garage, in the suburban bungalow.

I tried a number of scams to get a peek into the garage, none of which I care to mention here. In any event, all of them failed. However, I'd noticed a house for sale across the street and a couple of houses down from the bungalow, which offered a good view of the garage. I called on the realtor, showed him my detective's license, and gave him a moderately accurate idea of what I was doing, without revealing which house I was interested in. He was intrigued by the cloak-and-dagger aspect and let me use the house.

It was great. A house has enormous advantages in that you are usually less physically restricted, you are spared any struggle with the weather, and you have access to the facility most coveted by detectives—a toilet.

I was only there for about thirty hours when the owner of the bungalow opened the garage door and gave me the chance to make some lovely photographs of two gleaming motorcycles. The photos were enough to pry the location of the other motorcycles from the husband and to convince him to be somewhat more generous in the property settlement.

There are occasions when I'll use a restaurant, bar, or diner as a secondary spotting location. Obviously, you must have a table beside a window. If you order food, order a soup or salad or some other item that won't require a long preparation time. And be prepared to pay in cash—you may not have time to deal with credit cards. Don't pay at the register, even if it means leaving an obscenely large tip. Remember, every minute you spend away from the surveillance means you could be missing something.

Spotting Locations. A spotting location is the place from which you conduct the surveillance. There are both primary and secondary spotting locations. The primary location is where you'll spend most of your time. If possible, it should be selected before beginning the surveillance. It should be close enough to the object of the surveillance for you to see it plainly, but far enough away so that you aren't obvious.

Secondary locations are those that aren't quite as good as the primary location, but which allow the detective to shift around from place to place. Usually I look for secondary locations that get me out of the car. A diner with a convenient window, for example, or a stoop where rummies hang out.

It's also helpful to have a secondary parking location. This can be risky, however, in that you can't focus your attention on the object of surveillance while you're moving your car. Every minute you shift your attention from the object increases the chance that you'll miss something important.

Good spotting locations are far more difficult to find in the suburbs. Suburbanites tend to notice strange vehicles in their neighborhoods and are more willing to notify the police. In the suburbs, I try to park my car near the property line between two houses. That way people at each house tend to think the car is somehow connected with the other house.

Concealment. When conducting a surveillance from my car, I usually recline the seat until I can just see above the dashboard. I generally wear a baseball cap, which I pull down to conceal my eyes. Then I sit very still. If a passerby notices me, they think I'm napping. Oddly enough, however, people rarely seem to notice. I've parked on busy streets, in convenience-store and restaurant parking lots, even in the driveways of college students' houses, without being noticed.

I'm convinced that sitting very still is the key to escaping notice in a car. Movement attracts attention. You'll learn more about this in the section on the internal aspects of surveillance.

On foot, you can escape notice by blending in with the other people on the street. Unlike surveillance from a car, you can't stay still very long on foot. Merchants in the area tend to notice loiterers and get suspicious. That could mean a visit by the police, wondering what you're up to.

The only exception to this is if you can find a natural way to avoid notice. On more than one occasion I've bought a pint of vodka and joined a group of rummies on the street. (They get the pint; I drink soda out of a paper bag.) They're always glad to get a pint, and they provide excellent cover. People avoid looking directly at homeless people and drunks.

Breaking Off

Deciding when to terminate a surveillance is a judgment call. It depends entirely on the situation. And since no two situations are ever the same, I can't give you any solid rules about when to break off a surveillance. I can, however, give you some general guidelines.

Break off the surveillance:

1. If you have or think you might have been made. You can always try again. The O'Hara rule—tomorrow is another day—applies here.
2. If you've attracted any sort of unwanted attention, or if a disturbance happens nearby. A cop questioning you about loitering, for example, or maybe some street person panhandling nearby. Even if you don't think your subject noticed, don't take the chance. Better safe than sorry, if you'll pardon the cliché.
3. About an hour after you're absolutely, totally, without-a-doubt certain your subject is in for the night.
4. Whenever you feel the risk might be getting too high. Any sort of risk—the risk of getting made, the risk of getting mugged, the risk of falling asleep. Don't wait until you *know* the risk is too high. Break off when you feel it might be getting there.

Use your common sense. Unless you are under the pressure of a deadline, or unless you think something critical is about to happen, don't take any unwarranted chances. Break off and try again later.

On the other hand, don't be overly timid. Shakespeare said, "He is not worthy of the honeycomb that shuns the hive because the bees have stings." That's the Elizabethan way of saying "Got no guts, get no glory."

If you think there's a chance your subject might leave after you've broken off the surveillance, put a cheap watch under one of the subject's tires. When he drives away, he'll smash the watch. You can recover the watch in the morning; the hands of the watch will tell you what time the subject left. You may not know *where* the subject went, but at least you'll know what time he left to go there.

I actually learned that trick from the movie *Chinatown*. It's the only practical investigative technique I've ever seen on film. I've never had the occasion to use it, but I believe it will work. In any event, it's such a great scam that I have to pass it along. Just be certain you don't use a digital watch.

INTERNAL ASPECTS

When conducting a surveillance, you may be required to watch a certain location for hours without respite. During that time you cannot allow yourself to be distracted, either by some nearby activity or through tedium. You may have to disregard weariness, to distance yourself from your bodily needs. You may need to ignore discomfort, bug bites, muscle cramps, headaches, anything that might divert your attention.

How is that done?

Of all the factors influencing the success of a surveillance, the mental process is the most demanding. It's also the hardest to discuss. For a group of people whose livelihood depends on their ability to observe, analyze, and explain, detectives are remarkably nonintrospective. They seldom seem to indulge in self-examination.

I've asked other detectives how they manage to stay alert despite everything. I always get vague answers. "I don't know; I just *do* it."

I can try to tell you how I do it. Maybe it'll help you. Maybe not.

I disconnect my brain from my body. I let my body drift away until it no longer seems to be connected to me.

Sound ridiculous? It sounds that way to me, too. But that's what I do. I position the car, lean the seat back to the point where my eyes are level with the dashboard, and pull my cap down to conceal my eyes. Then I shut down all unnecessary systems.

I find I become very aware of what's going on around me, but I feel totally unaffected by it. I see people walking, I notice the cars driving by, I hear airplanes flying overhead. It's as if my mind is connected, but my body is detached.

It took me a while to develop this ability, if that's what it is. At first I had to consciously relax my body. First the feet, then the legs, and so on. Now my body seems to relax on its own. Except for my tongue. Every hour or so I'm surprised to find my tongue has jammed itself solidly against the roof of my mouth.

I know this process sounds vaguely mystical. I feel foolish writing it down. But it works for me. And so I don't question it very much.

There you have it: the Tao of surveillance.

I represented an eighteen-year-old boy accused of vandalizing a car. The car, a Corvette, belonged to another teenager, a high school classmate of my client. This kid had stolen the heart of the girl my client loved. My client blamed the loss of her affection on the car. He felt she'd have been true to him if it wasn't for the Corvette. How could she resist a Corvette?

So one fine spring day I was in court with my client, facing a charge of malicious mischief, to wit: throwing black paint and sand on a 1978 Corvette, license number PRQ229. The prosecution's case was fairly short. The victim testified that my client had no authority to throw paint and sand onto his car, and he explained that he was dating my client's former girlfriend. The arresting officer testified that he'd decided to interview my client after learning about the girlfriend situation. During the interview, the officer had noticed black paint splattered on my client's shoes. I called only one witness—a man from the Department of Motor Vehicles. He'd brought a certified copy of the registration for the car that had been issued license number PRQ229. The registration was for a 1977 Dodge. My client was not charged with vandalizing a 1977 Dodge. The judge dismissed the case.

What had happened? Was this just another bureaucratic blunder? Not quite. The victim had sold his 1977 Dodge when he bought the Corvette. But he kept the license plate and put it on the new car. And he didn't notify the Department of Motor Vehicles. Why? Who knows why an eighteen-year-old kid does anything?

We came across the discrepancy by accident. Greg was doing what he calls the grunt work, checking the dreary details, following the paper trail. But in this case, the paper trail was the yellow brick road. It didn't lead to Oz, but it kept my client out of jail.

But he still lost the girl.

R.G.

Chapter 4

THE PAPER TRAIL

Information is the detective's stock in trade. That's one of the reasons people turn to detectives—to get information they either can't or don't know how to get themselves. How do detectives do it? Through the development and knowledge of information sources.

In this chapter you'll learn about some of the detective's information-gathering techniques. (We'll talk about computers and the Internet in Chapter 12.) You'll learn how to develop and nurture personal sources, and how to find your way through the maze of official documents. You'll also learn some tips regarding the etiquette of bribery. In addition, I'll give you a practical demonstration showing how easily you can gather a great deal of information about practically anybody.

Most information sources fit into one of two categories:

- Personal—information possessed by people.
- Archival—written information from books, files, official records, and the like.

A good detective needs to be familiar with both.

PERSONAL SOURCES

It is much more difficult to extract information from people than from documents.

If the information exists on paper, all it requires is knowing where to look and the patience to do the looking. Written information is just there, waiting to be looked at and used.

People, on the other hand, are much more complicated. They may have information you want, but be unwilling to share it with you. They may have the information and not even know it. They may *not* have the information, but they know where you can get it. Sometimes they're entirely ignorant of the information you want, but pretend they *do* have it. In a later chapter I'll discuss techniques of interviewing. In this chapter I want to show you how to cultivate people in certain information-rich positions—bartenders, police officers, clerks, and telephone operators, to name a few. These people are all sources of valuable information, information that is tough to get anywhere else. The difficulty is getting them to give it to you.

How do you do it? You nurture a relationship with them. You make an effort to know them, to show some interest in them, to care about them. It's odd; but when you make that effort, you often find that you actually *do* come to care about these people.

People tend to respond to genuine interest. They tell you things, or help you find the information you want, or point you in the right direction.

I recall having to interview eight or nine nurses for a criminal case. They worked different shifts and in different departments. It might have taken me weeks to catch them all and interview them. But I'd taken the time on a previous case to be friendly with the nursing supervisor. I'd sent her a thank-you note after the case was over and a letter to her supervisor praising her for her assistance. Since she remembered me, she arranged for all the nurses to be at the hospital at a specific time and provided me with an office where I could speak to them individually.

Cultivating relationships can make the difference between success and failure. How is it done? Let's say you want to establish a relationship with a records clerk in city hall and a bartender at a local pub. There are four steps you need to consider:

1. Your purpose
2. Your target
3. Their usual audience
4. Your approach

I realize this sounds cold-blooded. It *is* cold-blooded. But the fact that you have an ulterior motive when you approach these people does not preclude your learning to like them. And if it turns out, after you've cultivated their friendship, that you *don't* like them—well, it's a cold-blooded business. Get used to it.

Consider your purpose. Why do you need to cultivate a clerk in city hall? Why a bartender in that particular bar?

The clerk may work in the tax assessor's office. Although there is a great deal of public information there, the clerks are often too busy or unwilling to help you with it. A friend in the tax assessor's office can save you a lot of time. A bonus is that city hall staff members often know each other. A clerk in one department is often familiar with clerks in other departments. A friendly introduction can get you places you couldn't reach on your own.

The bartender? Let's say he works at a trendy bar, one where people go to meet and discuss business. A bartender who knows who is talking to whom, or who is sleeping with whom, can be a valuable asset.

Consider your target. What sort of person is likely to become a clerk in city hall? The job is usually poorly paid and often monotonous. In other words, it's the type of job women are so often forced to take. We can safely assume the clerk is a woman. She could be of any age, but is likely to be married. She is probably overworked and underpaid. Her feet probably hurt and she is worried about gaining weight, but still takes pride in her appearance. She quietly resents being thought of as a mere extension of the typewriter.

The bartender, on the other hand, is probably male. He likes people, or he wouldn't have become a bartender. He's probably between twenty-one and thirty years old and likes to think he is wise in the ways of a wicked world. If he's working in a trendy bar, he's likely to be somewhat self-centered, a little arrogant, something of a showman. He probably likes money and the fast life.

Consider their usual audience. The people most clerks encounter are in a hurry. They want something, and they want it *now.* They're often rude, demanding, and impatient. A city clerk, to many citizens, is the most common manifestation of a bureaucracy they see as mindless or malevolent. They tend to treat clerks as if they were semi-intelligent and uncooperative stamp machines.

The bartender's audience is slightly different. Bar customers are usually more pleasant than those waiting to talk to a city clerk, but they still treat the bartender as a sort of servant. Most people have no idea how difficult it is to run an efficient bar, how tough it is to handle unruly customers without a scene. Some customers become intoxicated, which can make them aggressive, obnoxious, lecherous, maudlin.

Consider your approach. A good detective bases his approach on what the subject would like to see. What sort of person would a city hall clerk or a bartender in a trendy bar like to encounter? A polite, cheerful, friendly person.

Let them grow accustomed to your smiling face. Go to

the city hall fairly often. If you don't actually need anything, pretend you do. Always chat with the clerk for a
while. It doesn't matter what you chat about—the
weather, children, anything that's not controversial. All
that matters is that you are patient and pleasant. Clerks
rarely see pleasant faces. Always thank her for her help,
even if she didn't actually provide any.

Do the same at the bar. Go there often, but go before
it gets crowded. Don't sit at a table, take a stool at the
bar. You don't have to drink a lot; you don't have to drink
at all (again, there is the club soda with a twist of lime
dodge). Chat with the bartender. Don't interrogate him,
or quiz him. Just have a simple chat. Talk about sports
or ask about the bar. Or just shake your head and say,
"Boy, I bet you've seen some things working here." If he's
not busy, he's likely to tell you bar stories. All bartenders
have bar stories; most of them are worth listening to.
Leave him a gracious tip when you leave. Not an osten-
tatious tip, but a somewhat generous one.

As you can see, it takes time to cultivate a worthwhile
relationship. But, in the long run, it usually makes the
job easier and gives you access to information you
couldn't ordinarily get.

Once you've cultivated a source, you don't have to go
back as often. But you must still visit occasionally. They
have to see your friendly face.

I make rounds, like a doctor. Every three to five weeks,
I take an evening and visit a number of bars. I make sure
the bartender and the wait staff see my face, even if I
don't talk with them. I order a beer, take a few sips, chat
a bit, maybe read a chapter from my book, leave a good
tip, and go to the next bar.

I do the same with all my sources. It's like maintaining your car. You change the oil every three months.

Remember, all these clerks and secretaries and
mechanics and bartenders are important. These people

run the world. If they don't do their jobs, everything comes to a crashing halt. Treat them with warmth and courtesy, treat them as if they're important. They'll remember you and like you. And they'll help you.

There are no guarantees, of course. Sometimes all the charm and friendliness in the world won't get you anywhere. What then?

Bribery.

There's an old saying: "Money talks; bullshit walks." Like so many old sayings, it's only partially accurate. Bullshit is almost always enough. But there are times when the judicious application of cash can work wonders.

Bribery of public officials—and a records clerk could be considered a public official—is a crime. I have to advise you not to commit a crime. But on those occasions when an offer to make a person's pockets a little heavier is appropriate, here are a few simple rules:

1. *Be discreet.* Without fanfare and without looking at it, put the money where your target can see it and reach it. I've never been able to pull off the palming technique you see in the movies, but you may have better luck.

2. *Don't mention the money.* Say something like, "I really need this information." Your target will know what the money is for.

3. *Don't be cheap.* This is no time to economize. Offering any bill less than a twenty is an insult. Think in terms of multiple twenties and fifties.

4. *Don't gloat.* If your target takes the cash, don't let that "I knew you could be bought" look cross your face.

5. *Accept a refusal gracefully.* Smile shamefacedly. Apologize. Then get the hell out of there.

I realize this is a little sordid. And it's my experience that a good detective rarely needs to resort to crossing palms. But let's not be naive. If you decide you need to offer up a bribe, do it right.

ARCHIVAL SOURCES

There are only two requirements involved in finding archival data: knowing where to look and patience. I can't teach you to be patient. But I *can* show you where to look.

In the back of this book is a list of the major sources of archival information and the types of information that can be obtained from each source. What I'll do in this section is give you an idea about how the search for archival data is conducted.

Archival trails come in two varieties:

- Personal—the public information available regarding individuals.
- Property—the public information available regarding property.

I'll introduce you to both.

The Personal Trail

The best way to learn a thing is by doing it. You can't learn to ride a bicycle by following instructions in a book. Learning to follow a trail of public information is much easier than learning to ride a bicycle, but the same principle applies.

I'm going to give you an assignment. (If it helps, think of it as a case.) Then I'll walk you through a similar hypothetical case. The investigation we're going to make shouldn't take more than eight hours if you schmooze the clerks properly.

> *Assignment:* OPEN YOUR TELEPHONE BOOK AT RAN-
> DOM. PICK A NAME. FIND OUT EVERYTHING YOU CAN
> ABOUT THIS PERSON.

Don't panic. I'm going to show you what to do. This isn't going to be as difficult as it sounds. Trust me. When you're done, you'll be surprised at how easy it is.

All the material we gather is going to be public information. Although it is collected and stored by various state and local bodies, the information is there for you. But you have to ask for it. Sometimes you have to remind those in charge of the data that they're obligated to give it to you. But it's yours by right.

Here we go. We open the telephone book and this is what we see:

DOE, JOHN 1234 ADAMS ST.........123-4567

Not very original, I grant you, but it will do for our purposes.

Our first step is to go to the library. On the way we drive by 1234 Adams Street to look at John Doe's home. It's a small ranch-style house in a quiet, working class neighborhood. The yard is neat and we can see a chain-link fence enclosing the back yard.

At the library we ask for the city directory. Every city, and most towns, have a book called the city directory. This is not a telephone book. It's a book published by private companies. The city directory cross-indexes the city's residents by name, address, and telephone number. If Mr. Doe has been living in the city for a while, he will probably be listed. The listing will look something like this:

DOE, JOHN S (STEPHANIE R, PERKINS HARDWARE) 4Ⓗ
CALEDONIA ENTERPRISES. 1234 ADAMS ST. 123-4567

This tells you John Doe is employed at Caledonia
Enterprises. He is married to Stephanie R. Doe, who
works at Perkins Hardware. There are four people living
at his address—presumably John, Stephanie, and two
children. The circle with the letter "h" in it indicates Doe
owns, or is buying, the house at 1234 Adams Street.

The city directory increased our knowledge of John
Doe only marginally. But it gives us a base of information on which we can build. It widens the area of search.

Our next stop is city hall. At the motor vehicle department, we ask the clerk to check for automobiles registered to either John or Stephanie Doe. We learn John
Doe drives a blue 1996 Chevy Blazer, license number
32390A3. Stephanie drives a yellow 1989 Toyota Corolla,
with a vanity license plate reading STEVIE. We also learn
John owns a seventeen-foot Boston Whaler. (Boats have
to be licensed in most states.)

Down the hall at the tax assessor's office (the tax assessor determines the value of property and imposes a
property tax), we ask the clerk for the records regarding
Mr. Doe's property. The information may be listed either
by the address or by the name of the person paying the
tax. We find out that the house at 1234 Adams Street is
listed under John Doe's name. An assessed value is
recorded for the property. (Don't confuse the assessed
value of a property with its full market value; the
assessed value is usually a quarter to one half of the
actual market value—the assessment factor will either
be listed or can be determined by asking a clerk.) John
Doe has paid his property taxes. No other property is
listed to either John or Stephanie.

At the voter registration office we ask to see the voter
registration card for both John and Stephanie. John is

registered as a Democrat, while his wife is an Independent. The card also lists their birthdays. John was born on January 4, 1950; Stephanie was born a year later on August 13th.

Our picture of John Doe is beginning to fill out. We know he is married and has a family. It's reasonable to guess that he and his wife bring home moderately comfortable incomes from their jobs since they own two cars and a boat, as well as their house. We can speculate that they have two children. And we can safely assume Stephanie Doe prefers to go by the nickname Stevie.

Next we go to the county courthouse. At the marriage license section of the county recorder's office (or in the office of vital statistics), we ask the clerk for John and Stevie's application for a marriage license. We learn John Doe and Stephanie Roe were married on June 12, 1972. The marriage certificate also tells us the names and addresses of John and Stevie's parents, as well as their mothers' maiden names. We also get a look at both John and Stevie's signatures. The names of the witnesses, who were probably either relatives or very good friends, are also listed.

At the same office, in the birth certificate section, we look to see if any children were born to Stevie. We find Peter Doe was born January 21, 1973. His sister, Theresa, was born on June 2, 1975.

At the county clerk's civil office we ask the clerk if either John or Stevie has been involved in any lawsuits, or if any liens have been placed on their property. None are recorded. We do learn, however, that John was married once before—to Alice Desmaris. They were divorced in 1969.

At the criminal section of the county clerk's office we ask if either John or Stevie has any criminal charges pending, or if they have ever been indicted or tried for a crime in the past. Once again, there is no record of any such involvement.

Our next stop at the courthouse is the office of the county recorder (sometimes called the register of deeds). This is where all property transactions taking place in the county are recorded. The county recorder keeps an index book listing the names of those who have purchased or sold property. The index is by calendar year. The person who sold the property is referred to in the index, and on the deed, as the grantor. The person who purchased the property is called the grantee.

By searching under John Doe's name in each yearly index we learn that he purchased the house at 1234 Adams Street in 1973. We also learn how much the property cost and who he bought it from. He had a twenty-year mortgage with the First National Bank.

Our final stop is the probate office. Although we assume John and Stevie Doe are still alive, we can check on their parents. (Remember, we found their names on the marriage license.) Nothing is recorded for Stevie's family, but we discover John's father died in November of 1972, leaving him a tidy sum.

In three stops we've learned a great deal about John Doe, and we can conjecture more. We know John was married and divorced at the age of nineteen. We know he remarried and can guess that his second marriage was at least hastened by Stevie becoming pregnant (check the dates). We can further guess that John's inheritance from his father allowed him to make a down payment on the house, an uncommon extravagance for most young newlyweds expecting a baby.

Can we learn more? Of course. We don't know anything about his employment history, or any medical problems, or his credit rating. We don't even know what he looks like. Does he have hobbies? Does he drink? And after we know all those things, there will be still more to learn, and more after that.

In order to obtain a more complete picture of John

Doe, we have to go beyond the paper trail. We have to interview people—his neighbors, his coworkers, and his former employers. (Interviewing techniques are covered in Chapter 7.) We'd also be wise to examine Doe's trash (also covered in Chapter 5).

The best way to learn your way through the sea of public information is to wade in and swim. You'll probably be nervous the first time you approach a clerk in city hall and ask for information about a total stranger. I was. But, as I said, it's public information. You have a right to it. Some clerks, especially those in smaller towns, may not know the information is public. They may give you a hard time, but you have the right. It's up to you to exercise it.

The Property Trail

There is nothing sexy about following the property trail. It is dull, tedious work. But it can be vitally important.

There are two types of property: real property and personal property. Personal property is the stuff you own—cars, refrigerators, computers, and such. Real property refers to land and buildings. We're only concerned with real property.

People who own a lot of real property are usually people with a lot of power and influence. They're often a shy lot, especially when something shady is going on. And, since ownership of large parcels of real property can so often be equated with money and power, something shady is often going on. We ought to know who these people are.

The property trail is equally useful whether you want to uncover a slumlord or find out who is putting up the house on the corner lot. Again, the information is public and yours by right.

As before, I'm going to give you an assignment and then walk you through a similar hypothetical case. This assignment could be easier or more difficult, depending on your unique circumstances.

> *Assignment:* AT RANDOM, PICK A BUILDING IN THE NEAREST DOWNTOWN AREA AND FIND OUT WHO OWNS IT.

If you are very energetic, you could then use the techniques covered earlier in this chapter and find out everything you can about the person, or persons, who own the property.

Let's pick the quaint, four-story office building that houses our favorite bookstore. Its address is 5561 Dogbone Avenue.

Each state and city has its own unique method for collecting and recording property information. Fortunately, there's always a general resemblance between the systems. The names of individual agencies may differ, but the nature and purpose remains the same. If you are uncertain what the agency in your community is called, contact city hall and describe the type of information you want. They'll tell you the name of the proper agency to approach.

Our first stop is the city tax assessor's office. There we examine a series of maps showing each building in the city. From the map, we obtain a reference number that corresponds with a logbook containing the property information for that map section. (In many tax assessor offices, this process will be done by a clerk at your request.) The logbook tells us that the taxes for the property at 5561 Dogbone Avenue were paid by Amalgamated Management Systems Inc., located at 933 Houston Street. We also learn the value at which the property on Dogbone Avenue is assessed.

We check the name Amalgamated Management Systems Inc. in the telephone directory, but find no listing for it. A call to directory assistance is equally fruitless.

We drive to the Houston Street address given us by the tax assessor and find a small office building. The name on the door, however, is not Amalgamated Management Systems Inc., but Windom Enterprises.

Our next stop is the corporate division of the Secretary of State (not the U.S. Secretary of State—each individual state has its own Secretary or a similar office). There we ask to examine the articles of incorporation for Amalgamated Management Systems. (It is, remember, an incorporated entity, hence the "Inc." in the name.) From the articles of incorporation we discover the names of the AMS Inc. board of directors: Eliot Goodwin, Esther Madison, and Douglas Windom. A familiar name.

A similar search of the records for Windom Enterprises determines that Douglas Windom is the company president. It also reveals that Esther Madison is on the board of directors of Windom Enterprises.

We next stop by the county courthouse to check with the clerk of court regarding any criminal or civil litigation involving AMS Inc., Windom Enterprises, or any of the people we know to be associated with those companies. We find nothing.

While we are at the courthouse, we visit the county recorder. This is the office, if you recall, where all property transactions are recorded. There we search the yearly general index for the names of any of the individuals or companies. We discover that Windom Enterprises owns several other properties in town.

Are we finished? Not even close. Any mention of any of the target names provides us with more to research. In addition, we know nothing about the relationship between the people who operate the companies. Each coveted piece of information leads us a little closer. Closer to what? I don't know. Maybe nothing. That's why we're investigating—to find out.

As you can see, the property trail can be a difficult one to follow. Most property trails are a lot less convoluted than the one I've presented here. But the level of complexity increases as the value of the property under investigation increases. The more powerful the people involved, the better they are at masking their business interests. Often—not always, but often—they mask their interests not just for the sake of privacy, but because they're hiding something. And that knowledge is the incentive for locking on, for persisting. Because whatever they're hiding is worth finding out.

These scenarios shouldn't be interpreted as the only way to get the job done. In each scenario I ordered the investigative steps in a fashion that seemed logical to me. You don't have to follow the same order, or even follow the same steps. This isn't like a recipe or the instructions for putting together a swing set. It's more like a scavenger hunt.

This is how detectives operate. We dig a little, make a few educated guesses, then dig a little more. And then, a little more.

I tried to trust. I never read my lover's journal. I wouldn't watch his windows, look in his address book, follow him. I saved those tactics for my professional life.

But when I was in his kitchen, I couldn't help myself. I studied his trash. Can he really be using sculpting gel, I thought, or has another woman been making herself at home? Has he been using pantyhose for household chores? Or committing robberies? Had I ever seen him peel an apple? But I let it go.

And then it was a sunny weekend afternoon in late fall, and in a burst of ecological good will we took all those Sunday newspapers to be recycled. I noticed an unfamiliar hand had worked the crossword. An hour of good detective work saved me a lifetime of cross-examination. Learn to look at what's left behind.

R.G.

Chapter 5

THE DETECTIVE AS ARCHAEOLOGIST

Often when I turn the television to an educational channel, I see people patiently scraping away the surface of some equatorial desert, looking for evidence of our distant ancestors. They're looking for bits of bone, worn out tools, broken pottery, the refuse of ancient cultures. In other words, they're looking for trash.

Archaeologists are detectives. They do what detectives do—pay attention to small details, think about them, note patterns, then piece the puzzle together in a logical sequence. It's effective whether your subject is a two-million-year-old *Australopithecus africanus* or a thirty-six-year-old accountant. An archaeologist examining a fragment of a stone tool can speculate on the lives led by the people who made the tool. A detective examining discarded charge card receipts can speculate on the life led by the person who made the purchases.

We've been told that we are what we eat. We're also what we throw away. Our trash reveals a great deal about us, the sort of people we are, the sort of lives we lead. It's a valuable, if distasteful, source of information for the detective. A peek into a person's trash is a peek into his life—or lives.

Legally, trash is fair game. The U.S. Supreme Court has said, in effect, that if it's in the trash, it isn't protected by privacy laws (*California* v. *Greenwood*). But be careful; the law in the individual states may not reflect the Court's opinion. It may be wise to check the law in your state prior to snatching trash. (You can do this over the Internet—covered in Chapter 12—or simply by calling the state law library and asking for the relevant section of the state statutes.) Or you can take the chance of being a test case for your state.

In any event, you *cannot* trespass on private property to snatch trash. Trespassing is a crime. *Don't do it!* Fortunately for detectives, most cities require trash to be put at curbside for collection. The curbside is not deemed private property, and any items left there are considered to have been abandoned. Many cities also require trash to be placed in plastic bags, another boon for the detective. Nothing is worse than a soggy paper bag of garbage splitting open in your car.

To waste management professionals (there really are such people), there are two types of refuse: trash and garbage. Most people use the terms interchangeably, but you should be aware of the difference. Garbage consists of the remains of food—corn cobs and pork chop scraps, for example. Everything else is trash—broken bottles, old toys, newspapers, cardboard containers, and so on.

For our purposes we can further divide refuse into two categories:

- Personal refuse—those items discarded at homes and apartments. It consists of both trash and garbage.
- Business refuse—those items discarded at offices and places of employment. It is mainly trash, primarily paper.

In order to inspect refuse it is first necessary to snatch it, to physically remove it from where it was left and transport it to a place for examination. Trash is much easier to snatch in suburbs than in cities. In order to snatch trash from specific apartments or offices in buildings, you must rely on others, a prospect no detective relishes. The more people who are involved, the more likely something will go wrong.

To snatch trash from apartment and office buildings, you need the cooperation of the building superintendent, the porter, or the cleaning staff. That usually means a bribe. For a small fee, a super or a janitor might be willing to set aside the trash desired.

If offering a bribe offends you (or seems too risky, or if you're on a limited budget) think about taking a job with the cleaning service. The problem with that tactic is that it requires time to arrange and, if the cleaning service is a large one, there is no guarantee you'll be assigned to the building in question.

THE OPERATION

Before we discuss what sort of information you can expect to cull from your subject's trash, let's consider the necessary steps of a successful snatch operation.

- Pre-snatch logistics
- The snatch
- Tools
- The examination site

And please, try to control the urge to crack jokes about investigating being a dirty business.

Pre-Snatch Logistics

After you've reached the decision to lift somebody's trash, give some thought to how you're actually going to do it. This may not be the raid at Entebbe, but a little forethought can save a lot of aggravation.

Find out when the trash is collected. The easiest way to find out is to call city hall. That's why they're there. They'll be able to tell you if the trash is collected by a public or private service. They'll also be able to give you the telephone number of the collectors. Tell them you're house-sitting for a few weeks and want to know the trash collection schedule. Be sure to find out both the day and approximate time of collection.

Armed with that information, you should case the site. Drive by the subject's house late the night before the trash is collected, or very early in the morning—3:00 A.M. is a good hour. Many people put their trash out at night to save them from having to get up early in the morning. If the trash is there, take it. Never waste an opportunity. If it's not there, you can at least familiarize yourself with the area.

If you're going to make the snatch at an hour when it is dark, be sure to turn off the dome light in your car. You don't want to illuminate yourself when you open the car door. And wear dark clothes. But don't get carried away, and whatever you do *don't* cork your face or use camouflage make-up. You're taking somebody's trash, not burgling a jewelry store. How would you explain the burnt cork on your face if you got stopped by the police for having a burnt-out headlamp?

Also, consider how you're going to transport the trash to the examination site. You may want to line the trunk of your car with plastic. There are some disgusting things in the garbage, and you don't want them to foul your car.

Another suggestion—don't eat a large breakfast beforehand. And don't plan on eating for a while afterward, unless you have a high tolerance for foul odors and a cast-iron stomach.

The Snatch

Regardless of your preparation, when you actually step out of your vehicle to make the snatch, you're going to feel conspicuous. You're going to feel like you're on center court at Wimbledon, and everybody is watching.

Despite that feeling, it's highly unlikely anybody is going to notice you. People tend to put their trash at the curb and then forget about it. How often do you see *your* garbage collectors?

Still, the snatch should be done discreetly. Leave the car door open after you get out; it's quicker and quieter. Act as if taking trash from the curb and stuffing it in your rear seat or trunk is a normal routine. Don't rush, don't cast guilty glances at the houses, don't drop anything. Just walk quickly but calmly, pick up the trash, put it in the car, and leave. It's that simple.

What should you do if you're spotted? Or worse, confronted? I don't know. It's never happened to me. There are no hard and fast rules for situations like that. You have to play it by ear.

I *can* give you some advice. If you're spotted, ignore it. Act as if the person wasn't there, even if that person is your subject. If you are confronted, I advise lying. Tell the person you're a researcher for the Department of Health and are doing spot checks to determine what sort of trash is being discarded.

Will it work? Who knows? Detective work is like the best jazz—it demands the ability to improvise, to think quickly and fluidly, to adapt to the unexpected. Do whatever you think will work.

If possible, take along a partner. It makes the snatch quicker if there are multiple bags, and you're less likely to be confronted if you're caught.

Tools

It's important to have the proper equipment when doing a trash search. It just makes everything easier. Take along:

- *Several pairs of plastic or rubber gloves.* There's usually a lot of nasty stuff in personal trash, things you don't want to touch. You should also be careful not to cut yourself on used razors and open tin cans. Business trash is usually much less messy.
- *Something to dull the stench.* If you must do the examination inside, you'll want to mask the smell. Aerosol sprays work well. A bandanna scented with vanilla or a scented oil and tied around your face is also effective.
- *A probing tool.* A chopstick is terrific, but a pencil will do—anything to poke through the chicken bones, sodden broccoli, and other garbage you'd rather not touch.
- *Fresh trash bags.* When you've finished the examination, you'll have to rebag the stuff and throw it away again.
- *A camera.* This is vital if you need documentation for any reason, as in a child custody case, for example.

Examination Site

Garbage stinks. If possible, locate a well-ventilated area for the examination. A field, a large garage with windows, or any place with a lot of space. Don't use your home or office unless you live or work by yourself—or *want* to live or work by yourself.

THE INFORMATION

The actual process of sifting through refuse can be tedious and is often repulsive. Fortunately for the detective, although not for the environment, most personal trash is packaging—the boxes and bags things are sold in. If you're not interested in the quality or quantity of the items purchased, most packaging can be shoved to one side.

As a general rule, unless you're looking for a specific item—a telephone bill, for example—you must examine everything you find in the trash. Pay attention. Nothing should be overlooked.

This is especially true of business trash. You must look at each piece of paper that's thrown away. Not just the letters, the invoices, and the receipts, but each piece of paper. People write notes on Post-its, on envelopes, on scrap paper, on napkins. A telephone number scribbled on a corner ripped from a yellow legal pad might be of vital importance. Pay close attention.

What can a person's trash tell you? More than they'd want you to know. You can gather a lot of information about your subject's

- Friends and family
- Finances
- Drinking or drug habits
- Diet
- Sexual behavior
- Physical and emotional condition

Trash talks.

Friends and Family

Unlike my mother, not everybody saves all the letters and cards they receive. Return addresses on envelopes can be helpful, and the contents of the letters can be very revealing. One of the best times to check for addresses is during holidays and for a few days afterward.

Discarded telephone bills are tremendously useful. They can provide you with the telephone numbers of your subject's long-distance friends and associates. The telephone numbers themselves can lead you to more information. If a subscriber can give his account number (which is listed on the bill) and the specific page of the bill where the telephone number is noted, the telephone company will provide the name of the person to whom the call was made. I'm not suggesting you lie to the telephone company and pose as the subscriber; I'm merely passing on the information.

Finances

A thorough search through the garbage can give you some idea of how and where a person spends his money. Look for discarded credit card receipts, overdue or late bills, letters from collection agencies. Automatic teller receipts are always dated, usually provide the address where the transaction took place, and often include a notation of the owner's current balance. Check for crumpled-up lottery tickets. Look inside discarded shopping bags—when people purchase things they often throw away the receipts with the bag. In addition, a surprising number of people throw away their paycheck stubs.

Drinking or Drug Habits

Your subject's drinking habits can sometimes be determined from the trash. Count the number of bottles and
note the brands. This not only tells you how much the
subject drinks, but how much he spends on alcohol.

Search for the detritus of hangover nostrums. Look
for the ends of celery stained with tomato juice (used for
Bloody Marys) and empty bottles of Gatorade (used as
fluid replacement for alcohol dehydration). But don't
forget that Gatorade is also used by athletes, so it is sig-
nificant only when found in conjunction with other
signs of heavy drinking.

Look for matchbooks to discover if the subject hangs
out in bars. Always be sure to check the inside covers for
telephone numbers and addresses.

The use of illegal drugs is more difficult to detect.
Examine discarded plastic bags for marijuana seeds and
stems. Note any small vials, which are popular cocaine
and crack containers. Look for triangular scraps of
paper that might have been used as cocaine bindles.
Corners of magazine pages are popular bindles; they
hold a crease well, have smooth surfaces, and lie flat in
the pocket.

Diet

Diet sometimes becomes an issue in child custody cases.
Courts are often interested in how much junk food a
child eats, and the trash can show the sort of meals the
child eats at home. Simply noting the garbage can help
determine if the child exists on a diet of Spaghetti-Os
and frozen dinners or home-cooked meals with fresh
fruit and vegetables. Many grocery stores now have

computers that itemize groceries by brand name and price on the receipt; you can often find the receipts inside discarded grocery bags.

Sexual Behavior

Investigating a person's sexual behavior is distasteful, but there are times when it's important. And even if you aren't specifically interested in your subject's sexual habits, a detective can never have too much information. Knowing your subject's menstrual cycle might also somehow come in handy.

Contraceptive methods can be determined from empty tubes of spermicidal foam, foil condom packages, and discarded containers for birth control pills. Check wadded tissues for used condoms. In a man's trash, empty tubes of K-Y or petroleum jelly might indicate homosexual activity, as could a lot of laxative packages. Look for bottles that contained scented or flavored oils.

Special sexual interests can sometimes be determined from discarded magazines and newsletters. If alternative newspapers are found, check the personal sections for circled advertisements.

Again, pay attention, examine everything, and *think*. It never hurts to think.

Physical and Emotional Condition

Evidence of every malady from chronic aches and pains to full-blown psychotic episodes can be found in the trash. Look for discarded pill containers and medicine bottles. Make note of over-the-counter medicine packages or bottles—antacids, analgesics, sleeping aids, etc. They can tell you a lot about the subject's general health.

On prescription containers, note the name of the drug, the dosage, the number of pills issued, and the doctor's name. The *Physician's Desk Reference* at the public library can tell you what the drug is, what medical problems it is used to treat, and what the contraindications are. You can also obtain this information online (see Chapter 12).

If you're covering a person's trash over a period of time and notice a marked decrease in the amount of food being consumed, it could indicate emotional distress. (It could also indicate a new diet—look for other signs of distress.) A lot of damp tissues could mean that the subject has been crying a lot, or simply that the subject has a cold.

To summarize, everything that gets thrown away can tell the careful observer something about the person who throws it away. Everything that gets cast aside has a message. All you have to do is make the effort to find it and understand it.

One of the first things lawyers learn is not to ask too many questions. When I'd send Greg out to find a witness or a missing client, I never asked how he did it. It was enough for me that he did.

Then one day, I wanted to mail a letter to some friends, but I couldn't recall their address. I didn't have my address book with me, and I didn't want to go home to get it. Suddenly, I was helpless. I had no idea how to find my own friends.

So I did the smart thing. I asked a detective.

Greg made a few suggestions and handed me the telephone. Five minutes later I had the envelope addressed.

Since that time I've been able to discover the address of the man who put the dent in my fender. And the address of a city council member who was avoiding a subpoena. And the address of the guy at the gym.

This stuff comes in handy.

R.G.

Chapter 6

HOW TO LOCATE JUST ABOUT ANYBODY

People today seem to come and go like tumbleweeds. Rootless, they drift along, attracting little attention and leaving few signs they were ever there. Close friends move across town and disappear out of our lives. Family members lose touch with each other with alarming ease. Lovers argue, separate, and fade away.

Where do they all go? How can you find them? How do you locate a witness to an accident, for example, or to a crime? How can you track down a person who owes you money? If friends and family are so difficult to keep track of, how can anybody hope to find near strangers?

In this chapter you'll learn how to track people down. You'll be given some general guidelines on the techniques for locating people and, through the use of scenarios, you'll be shown how to put those guidelines to use.* Locating people combines the best and the worst aspects of detective work. Sometimes it's tedious and monotonous, requiring hours of dreary footwork. Other times it demands creativity and elaborate cleverness.

A few years ago, I was asked to locate a certain doctor. He'd been present in the emergency room while the police interrogated a man suspected of an attempted

---

* A related but separate issue involves adopted children searching for birth parents, and birth parents searching for the children they gave up for adoption. Information on this topic can be found in Appendix C.

murder. There was some question about the voluntari-
ness of the man's statement to the police. The doctor, I
was told, might be able to shed some light on the matter.

The only information I was given was the doctor's sur-
name (say, Smith) and the fact that he'd worked in the
ER of a certain small town hospital on a certain night
six weeks before. The town was located near the border
of two New England states, and the hospital served communities in both.

It didn't seem like a tough assignment. I had nurtured
a good relationship with one of the nursing supervisors
at that hospital, so I called her. She was able to check the
emergency room schedule and tell me the doctor's full
name—Kevin Smith. Unfortunately, Dr. Smith wasn't on
the ER schedule for the next two weeks.

The nursing supervisor also told me that the hospital
often hired doctors from other areas to cover the ER on
week nights. Those temporary doctors sometimes only
worked one night every two weeks. Dr. Smith was apparently one of those doctors. She didn't have access to the
personnel records, so she couldn't give me any more
information.

I called the ER and said I needed to talk to Kevin
Smith. I asked for him by name, as if I knew him, and I
used that curt tone of voice used by doctors who are
accustomed to being obeyed. The nurse told me what I
already knew, that Dr. Smith wasn't there. I thanked her
and said I'd call him at his office. As if it was an after-
thought, I asked her if she had "Kevin's" other work number handy. She did. And she gave it to me without asking
any questions. The area code was for the other state.

I called the number and learned it was for an internal
medicine clinic in a town about thirty miles from the
border. When I asked for Dr. Kevin Smith, I was told he
no longer worked there. He had resigned a month earlier. The receptionist said she had no idea where he was

currently employed. She didn't know whether he still lived in the area. No, she wouldn't give me the address or telephone number she had listed for him. She was sorry she couldn't help, but rules are rules, and they were very busy, thank you for calling, goodbye.

I'd run into a dead end, but I wasn't too discouraged. I was a detective, after all, and I had all the detective's tools at my disposal. I reached for the telephone book for that area. In the yellow pages, under "Physician," Dr. Kevin Smith was listed. Unfortunately, the only listing was under the clinic's number, the one I had just called. There was no listing for Kevin Smith in the white pages.

I called directory assistance for the communities surrounding the town where the clinic was located and found four Kevin Smiths. I called each of them, but none was a doctor.

I called all the internal medicine clinics in that area. No Kevin Smith.

More dead ends. But I still wasn't discouraged. It only meant I'd have to leave my office to find Dr. Kevin Smith.

I went to the public library and looked up Kevin Smith in the *American Medical Directory*. That gave me the name of the school he'd attended and the year he graduated, as well as the name of the clinic where he had been employed. By looking through a few other listings for the same area I found the names of two other doctors who had attended the same medical school at the same time as Dr. Smith.

While I was at the library, I also checked the city directory for the community in which the clinic was located. No listing for Dr. Kevin Smith.

Back at my office, I began to work the telephone. I called the medical school, giving one of the other doctor's names, and saying I was trying to locate my old buddy Kevin. The secretary at the alumni center had an address for him, and kindly supplied it to me. It was the address of the clinic where Smith no longer worked.

I called both the doctors, saying I was from the alumni center and looking for Dr. Smith. Neither of them had seen him since getting out of medical school.

I called the nearest chapter of the American Medical Association; they only had the clinic address. I called half a dozen medical journals to see if they'd received a change of address. Dr. Smith received only one of the journals, and it was delivered to the clinic.

I was beginning to get discouraged. I asked myself where, besides a hospital or clinic, a doctor would spend his time. I opened the telephone book again and began to call golf courses and country clubs in the area. I called fitness centers, racquet clubs, and gyms. Nothing, nothing, nothing.

By now I was definitely discouraged. But I was a detective, after all, with all the detective's tools at my disposal. I drank a beer and threw darts for forty-five minutes. Everybody has his own method for clearing his mind.

Finally, I got an idea. I called the clinic again. This time I identified myself as a representative of a well-known computer company. I said we'd received a number of complaints about keyboards from customers who had purchased a certain model of computer and we'd been authorized by the company to replace those keyboards free of charge. I said I had Dr. Smith's new keyboard and asked when he wanted it delivered.

I have no idea if Dr. Smith even owned a personal computer. But I thought it was the sort of expensive, high-tech contraption a doctor might own, and I surmised the receptionist would be equally ignorant. It didn't seem likely, though, that she'd refuse to cooperate with a person offering a free replacement part for a complex and expensive piece of electronic equipment.

I didn't ask to speak with Dr. Smith, and I didn't give the receptionist a chance to tell me he wasn't there. I just gave my little rap and asked when the keyboard should be delivered. I didn't ask *where* to deliver it, just when. I didn't want the receptionist to think I was concerned with *where*.

The receptionist explained that Dr. Smith no longer worked there and she didn't know where he'd gone. I said the offer was only good for a limited time. She hesitated, then put me on hold. A short time later, another doctor got on the line, a friend of Dr. Smith. Smith, I learned, hadn't moved; he'd simply joined the staff of a health maintenance organization. The doctor gave me Kevin Smith's new work address and telephone number as well as his home address and his unlisted home telephone number.

Piece of cake.

Given time, almost anybody can be tracked down. For the most part, the people that detectives locate aren't actively hiding. They just aren't where they were expected to be. They've switched jobs, moved, married, gone on vacation, joined a religious order. They've changed their lives in some way.

That change doesn't have to be drastic. Even a minor change in a person's life situation, over time, can have major effects. Physicists have a phrase for similar phenomena: "sensitive dependence on initial conditions." A small event can cause unpredictable and radical changes. And the longer the period of time from the event, the more radical the changes. A neighbor moves fifteen blocks away. He has a new set of neighbors, shops at new markets, and fills his prescriptions at a new pharmacy. It's inconvenient to see his old friends. People ask each other, "Whatever happened to old what's-his-name?" After twelve months, it's as if he'd never lived in the old neighborhood.

How can you find "old what's-his-name"? First, assume the project is going to take considerable time. It may not, but it's best to approach it as if it will. That gives you the proper pace. Endurance, attitude, and attention to detail should bring you through. In addition, tracking people will be easier if you remember a few basic tenets:

1. *Nobody lives in a vacuum.* People are interdependent. Most of us are connected to others in some fashion—through friendship, family ties, neighbors, coworkers. The more people you interact with, the easier it is to find you.

2. *People are creatures of habit.* It's easier to change your address, to change your career, even to change your appearance than it is to break a habit. Habits can be anything from the brand of cigarette you smoke or the games you play to the manner in which you dress. The more habits you have, the easier it is to find you.

3. *People are reluctant to change affiliations.* Democrats tend to remain Democrats, Methodists usually continue to attend a Methodist church, Red Sox fans will *always* have their hearts broken each fall. The stronger and more numerous your affiliations, the easier it is to find you.

4. *Few people are free from bureaucracy.* While it's true that an appalling number of people are homeless or live day to day by panhandling, most people still have utility bills. They still drive cars and pay rent and have debts. The more bureaucratic ties you have, the easier it is to find you.

Unless people are *actively* making an effort to disappear, they leave a trail. All you have to do is follow it.

Every attempt to locate somebody starts with what can be called a "guide." A guide is a solid piece of information the detective can seize hold of and work with. It could be a name, an address, a telephone number, any link with the subject. The guide will lead you in a certain direction. As you follow, you'll gather more information, more guides. It's a cumulative process and, eventually, one of those guides will lead you to the person you seek.

We'll examine three hypothetical scenarios to demonstrate how the process works. In each scenario, we'll begin with a different guide and follow it through to the end. Or to something like a conclusion.

Keep in mind that these scenarios are models. They aren't road maps for tracking people down. Rather, they're meant to be used as a compass, a tool to help you get your bearings. While reading them, try to think of other ways to get the same result. The result, finding the person you're after, is what really counts. There aren't any wrong paths—just different ways of getting there.

SCENARIO 1

WE ARE ASKED TO LOCATE A WOMAN NAMED DEBORAH HALPERIN. THE ONLY INFORMATION WE HAVE IS HER NAME AND A TWO-YEAR-OLD ADDRESS.

Obviously, our first move is to go to that address. She might still live there, after all. Not everybody moves like tinkers.

The address is an old house, partitioned into four apartment units. Unfortunately, Ms. Halperin doesn't live in any of them. (You didn't actually think she was going to be there, did you? What sort of exercise would that be?) The obvious next move is to talk to the neighbors. None of them, however, have lived in the building for more than a year. None is familiar with Halperin. We do, however, obtain the name and address of the building's landlord.

We go to see the landlord. He tells us Deborah Halperin moved out of the apartment around a year ago. She did not leave a forwarding address.* Fortunately, the landlord still has Deborah Halperin's rental application on file. Landlords are a cautious group of people and they ask a lot of personal questions on their applications, including such diverse questions as the applicant's place of employment, next of kin, and prior residence. Any such information is a useful guide.

Rental applications *are not* public documents. The landlord is under no obligation to show it to us. However, it's been my experience that landlords can usually be persuaded to help. How that's done is a matter of discretion. I suggest you tell the truth, if you think it'll work. A small monetary contribution might also be effective. (See Chapter 4 in regard to bribes.)

For whatever reason (whether out of the kindness of his heart or because we've made his pockets a little heavier), the landlord lets us examine the rental application. We learn that when she moved into the apartment, Deborah Halperin was employed by Big Rudy's Seafood Restaurant. We also get the name, address, and telephone number of her mother (as next of kin).

The mother is the obvious choice. Mothers almost always know where their children are. The difficulty is in deciding on the proper approach. While mothers usu-

---

* Until a few years ago, we could ask the local post office for a forwarding address. However, the post office no longer supplies that information—with a couple of exceptions. They'll give it out in response to written requests from process servers who are attempting to serve legal documents. And they'll turn forwarding addresses over to federal, state, and local law-enforcement agencies for official duty purposes and in response to court orders.

ally know where their children are, they're also protective; they'll want to know why *you* want to know where their children are. Do we go to the mother, knock on her door, and tell her who we are and what we want? Or do we call her on the telephone and run a scam on her, tell her we're an old friend of her daughter? Or some combination of the two approaches?

The choice of approach is normally related to the reasons you're looking for a person. Obviously, if you don't want the subject to know why you're looking for her (or even that you *are* looking for her), you make an oblique, subtle approach. For the purposes of this scenario, we'll assume our purposes are benign and that we have nothing to hide. Therefore, we go directly to the mother's house and knock politely on the door.

Mom sees our cheerful, smiling, honest face and gladly tells us her daughter Deborah is now living at the Wiltshire Apartments on Dodge Street. Apartment 210 West. Nothing to it.

But what if mom *hadn't* liked our cheerful, smiling face? What if she tossed us out on our ear? Are we out of luck?

Not at all. We can examine mom's trash, looking for signs of Deborah. We can conduct a surveillance of the house and tail every young woman who visits (assuming we don't know what Deborah Halperin looks like). We can wait a week and try some variation of the original plan of calling and scamming mom.

And if that doesn't work? We still have the restaurant mentioned on the rental application. If Halperin no longer works at Big Rudy's, we can check with her former coworkers. If they don't know where she currently lives or works, they might know the names of other friends who might know.

And if that doesn't work? We can start looking at the paper trail on Deborah Halperin. Does she have a car registered? Is she registered to vote? We can call the utility companies and ask if Deborah Halperin is a customer.

And if *that* doesn't work? Well, we'll think of something else.

SCENARIO 2

> OUR CLIENT HAS SEEN HIS WIFE GETTING OUT OF A BLUE SEDAN WITH LICENSE NUMBER P344002 AT TWO O'CLOCK ON THE PRECEDING FRIDAY AFTERNOON. WE ARE ASKED TO IDENTIFY AND FIND THE PERSON WHO WAS DRIVING THE CAR.

Our only guide is the license number. Most private detectives who've been in the business for a while have developed contacts who will run a check on license numbers. This is a luxury you probably don't have. So our obvious first step is to check with the Department of Motor Vehicles.

Each state and local DMV has its own unique rules regarding the distribution of information. Very few state agencies will provide you with the information over the telephone. Given the least opportunity, bureaucrats usually revert to type—they become petty, mean-spirited, and small-minded. They'll demand a written request detailing why you want the information. I suggest you approach the city motor vehicle registration office rather than the state DMV. City employees are usually more cooperative and more professional than their state counterparts, but even they can be difficult.

The police, of course, have almost instant access to motor vehicle information. However, there's little point in consulting the police, even if you have a legitimate reason for wanting the information. They're not in the business of tracing vehicles unless a crime is involved.

And if a crime is involved, they're unlikely to share the information with you.

The DMV, then, is your best bet. Your approach to the DMV will reflect your own personal style. I'll tell you the approach I use for those times I haven't been able to reach a contact to run a license check for me. You're welcome to use it, if it meets your ethical standards.

I lie. (Yes, I realize lying is not acceptable behavior in polite society. But polite society rarely needs to track people down. Do you want the information or not? You can rejoin polite society later.) I telephone the local DMV and lie to a clerk. The lie usually goes something like this:

> *I'm just traveling through town and I stopped at this drugstore for some aspirin. As I was getting out of my car, I saw this woman put a package on top of her car while she unlocked it. Then she got in the car and drove off, with the package still on top. It fell off as she was pulling out of the parking lot. It looks like a birthday present for a child. I tried to stop her, but she didn't hear me. But I got her license number. It's P344002 or 03. Can you tell me who owns the car?*

This is the bare bones, of course. But it gives you the idea. It shows you're a concerned and considerate person for wanting to return a lost birthday present; it demonstrates a sense of urgency, since you're just traveling through town; it gives the clerk every reason in the world to want to help you.

Of course, it doesn't have to be a woman who lost a birthday present. It could have been a student who lost a knapsack full of books, or an old man who dropped his bifocal sunglasses.

It's a good, functional, generic lie. We use it, and it works. We find that license number P344002 is registered as a blue 1986 Chevrolet belonging to Robert Jeffrey Delaney of 2323 Worsted Road.

Now we have to ask ourselves the important question. Is he our man? Was he driving his car last Friday at two o'clock in the afternoon?

Who knows? Delaney has to be interviewed. (Interviewing skills are discussed in a Chapter 7.) If he denies driving the car, then he should be able to provide us with other leads to follow. And as long as we have something to guide us, we're in business.

SCENARIO 3

> WE'RE ASKED TO FIND A MAN CALLED TWIST. THE ONLY INFORMATION WE HAVE ABOUT TWIST IS THAT HE USED TO HANG OUT AT A BAR CALLED THE MADISON GRILL A COUPLE OF YEARS AGO.

We check the telephone directory, but find no listing for the Madison Grill. We call directory assistance, but they have no listing either. We call the local police dispatcher. Police and fire department dispatch operators commonly have detailed maps and charts showing the location of every building in their precinct. The reason we called the police dispatcher rather than the fire department is because police officers are more familiar with bars. Bars are often the scene of trouble.

The police dispatcher tells us the Madison Grill closed over a year ago, but gives us its old address. We go there and find a boarded-up shell of a building that had obviously once housed a saloon for serious drinkers.

Our next stop is the Alcohol Beverage Control Board. Every state has an agency that regulates and enforces the liquor licensing laws. The agency also maintains records of the licenses that have been issued. The name of the agency, however, may vary from state to state. If you don't know—or can't find—the name of the agency in your state, call the general information telephone number listed for your state government. They'll tell you. Or call a bar and ask—whichever you're most comfortable with.

At the Alcohol Beverage Control Board, we ask for the name and address of the owner who was issued a license for the Madison Grill. You may hear the expression "DBA" used when talking with an employee of the Alcohol Beverage Control Board. DBA is an acronym for "doing business as." It's the name under which a business operates. In this particular case, the Madison Grill is the DBA.

We learn that the liquor license for the Madison Grill was issued to John McCormick. The liquor license has lapsed, but it includes McCormick's home address at the time he applied for the license.

From here on, it's grunt work—knocking on doors and asking questions. First we have to find McCormick. He may not know Twist, he may not know his real name, he may not know where he can be found. But he'll have the names of other Madison Grill employees, and *they* might know. Or they'll know the names of some of the bar's regulars, and *they* might know. One way or another, Twist will be found.

And that's how it works. You get one scrap of information and you grab it, then you work it until it reveals other scraps of information. Once the search for a person begins, it is more common to have too much information than too little. The difficulty is in knowing which scraps of information are likely to pay off.

As I said earlier, given enough time, almost anybody can be tracked down. All it takes is a little creativity, a little planning, a little attention, and a whole lot of persistence.

In the course of our investigations, Greg went down many mean streets and into many mean bars. He talked to violent men and women who believed in their right to bear arms and use them if riled. He spent hours alone with rapists and killers. Some were men behind bars who had nothing to lose. He went unarmed, and he returned unscathed. That's because people can be verbally seduced, if you know how.

Only one time did Greg come back with blood on his hands. He had, in self-defense, punched a rottweiler in the mouth. A rottweiler is a dog—a cross between a Doberman and a Jeep.

R.G.

Chapter 7

VERBAL SEDUCTION

Al Capone said you can get farther with a kind word and a gun than with a kind word alone. Big Al never would have made it as a detective. No subtlety.

And subtlety is what it takes to get information from a person who doesn't want to give it to you.

I had to interview a young woman whose husband had been badly injured in a fight. My information was that the fight took place as a result of a bad drug deal. Although I doubted the woman would want to talk to me (I was working for the man accused of putting her husband in the hospital), I felt I had to try to speak with her. She might know something about the events preceding the fight.

I went to her home and she invited me in. As I walked in, I noticed a bunch of educational toys for an infant. On a coffee table was a group of photographs, sitting on top of the envelope they came in. It looked as if she'd put them down to answer the door. A couple of library books on parenting were also in the room. Obviously, this was the adoring mother of a first child.

I explained who I was, who I worked for, and why I was there. (A good private detective never misrepresents himself on a criminal case—too much is at stake.) The woman frowned, obviously not happy to see me. As I was explaining, the child waddled into the room. She was about two years old and dressed in an expensive sleeper that I would have guessed was out of their price range.

Like all children, she didn't know any better than to avoid strangers. She walked straight up to me and demanded "up." So I picked her up and told her what a smart and pretty little girl she was. For a few moments I ignored the mother and spoke to the child. I sat on a hassock and gave her everything in my pockets that I thought might entertain her.

Once the child was happily playing with my car keys, I looked up and smiled at her mother. She was smiling back. I told her again who I was and why I needed to speak with her. I did *not* tell her how wonderful her daughter was. That could backfire; she might think I was saying it simply because I wanted to butter her up. Which, for the most part, was true. Instead, I let her *see* that I liked the child.

The woman sat down and answered my questions, while I continued to entertain and tickle her daughter. I interrupted her once or twice to make a face and a silly noise at the child. Then I asked mom to repeat what she had said, which she did happily.

After all, how could she refuse somebody who so obviously appreciated what an exceptional child she had?

Subtlety.

When conducting an interview, a good detective engages in a form of seduction—verbal seduction. He creates a mood designed to elicit the information he wants. He invites the subject to like him and trust him. He allows the subject to realize how singular and unique he or she is. And he provides the subject with an opportunity to speak and be heard. Verbal seduction is a total engagement of mind and body, the detective's and the subject's.

Verbal seduction, at its best, should appear spontaneous. And there *should* always be an element of spontaneity in an interview. But that spontaneity needs to be laid on a solid foundation of basic skills. In order to consistently get good interviews the detective needs:

- Good interpersonal skills
- Pre-interview preparation
- A way to get in the subject's door
- Familiarity with standard interviewing techniques
- An understanding of body language

Of course, you *can* get a good interview while being absolutely ignorant of these things. But you can't do it consistently. And consistency is what pays the bills.

INTERPERSONAL SKILLS

The interpersonal skills required to be a good interviewer are these:

- Good manners
- Flexibility
- An intuitive understanding of human nature
- Self-confidence

These skills are critical. We'll examine them all.

Good Manners. I realize that manners might seem an unlikely qualification for a detective. But don't confuse manners with the social graces. Good manners involves more than not chewing with your mouth open. The essence of good manners is putting other people at ease, making them feel comfortable, putting their wants before your own. A person who insists on the unconditional use of social graces may be well trained, but is not well mannered.

I want to stress the importance of putting people at their ease. People are usually more willing to give you information if they feel comfortable. Mata Hari, after all, didn't become a famous spy because of her ability as an interviewer. I'm not suggesting you sleep with a witness (a quick word of advice about sleeping with witnesses—*don't*), but I am suggesting you make every reasonable (and perhaps even unreasonable) effort to make your witness comfortable.

I had to interview a young couple who had witnessed an attempted murder. The couple and their two small children lived in a small, fetid mobile home that reeked of stale sweat, garbage, and dirty diapers. I'd come unannounced, and they were embarrassed at the slovenly condition of the trailer.

Despite their embarrassment they invited me in, asked me to sit, and offered me a cup of coffee. I didn't want to go in (it was summer and the trailer stank), I didn't want to sit (the chair was filthy), and I didn't want any coffee (I hate coffee). But good manners (and the job) required it. I went in, sat down, leaned back in the chair, and said I'd love a cup of coffee.

The husband had been working on a carburetor when I arrived. His hands were too greasy to hold the youngest child, so I offered to hold the baby while the wife poured the coffee. The child was wearing nothing but a cloth diaper that was saturated with feces.

I sipped the coffee and we chatted for a while about the heat and the difficulty keeping a house clean with two children. As they relaxed I slowly led the conversation into the crime they'd witnessed. By the time I was ready to leave, they were calling me by my first name.

When I got back to the office my clothes smelled of dirty diapers. My coworkers held their noses and avoided me. I had to go home and change clothes. That, too, was good manners.

Putting people at ease is usually critical for conducting a good interview. There *is* a time and place for rudeness, but we'll cover that later.

Flexibility. It's difficult to predict how a total stranger will behave. Each moment of an interview reveals something about the person being interviewed, what upsets or angers him, what he finds important or interesting. During an interview a good detective will constantly re-evaluate his view of the subject, and then act on the new evaluation. You must be able to rapidly adjust to that changing perspective. A good detective is something of a social contortionist—he bends and wiggles to match the subject.

An Intuitive Understanding of Human Nature. You can't put people at ease if you don't know what makes them comfortable. Fortunately, most of us have a fairly good intuitive feel for human nature. *Unfortunately*, we rarely put it to use.

We know people want to be believed. We know they want to be respected, to be genuinely understood and appreciated. A good detective, rather than spend all his time probing for information, will focus at least part of his concentration on understanding his subject. This is especially important at the beginning of the interview.

In most circumstances, your intuitive understanding of human nature, plus a little consideration, will give you enough insight into your subject to allow you to get the information you need.

Self-Confidence. Quiet self-confidence is a critical component of the detective's temperament. You have to believe in your ability to cope with any situation that arises. Don't confuse confidence with cockiness or a lack of caution. A cocky detective is a stupid detective, and stupid detectives don't stay in business.

Self-confidence communicates itself to witnesses. I always try to behave as if the person I want to talk to also wants to talk to me. It's rarely true, but if I *act* as if it's so, then sometimes people think it must be true. And then they answer my questions.

PRE-INTERVIEW PREPARATION

Marathon runners don't run without stretching first. Concert pianists don't perform without warming up first. Even Mike Tyson doesn't box without training first. So it should be no surprise that a good detective doesn't do an interview without preparing first.

The primary reason for preparation is to gain a degree of familiarity with the case. The more comfortable you are with the facts, the more comfortable you'll be during the interview. Give some thought to these suggestions.

Clarify Your Reasons for the Interview

Why do you need to talk to this person? What sort of information does he or she have? What sort of information are you looking for? This should seem obvious. But I once drove a couple hundred miles, found a missing witness, and did a great interview that seemed to set the stage for an insanity defense. It wasn't until I was back at the office that I remembered the lawyer I was working for was trying to have some evidence suppressed on the basis that the arrest had been illegal. At that point, the lawyer was more interested in information about the client's arrest than in a defense for the trial. There wouldn't even *be* a trial if the evidence was suppressed. But I was so jazzed about the insanity issue that I'd neglected to ask a single question about the arrest itself. I had to drive the two hundred miles all over again.

Review All Material about the Case

The more familiar you are with the facts, the easier the interview will be. You never know what tiny bit of information will turn the case around—a description of a car, the name of a tavern, anything. A weapons dealer once decided that I could be trusted just because I referred to a certain man by his nickname. The nickname was about all I knew about the man. But it was enough.

Think of a General Approach to the Witness

You'll approach a friendly witness differently than a hostile one. You'll want to approach a bank officer differently than a gas pump jockey. The more you know about the subject, the more you can narrow the approach, but by and large detectives usually have to approach a witness almost cold. So it's best to keep the approach general and be prepared to change it.

Don't Over-Prepare

This relates to the point I just made. While you can't have too much information about the case, it's possible to prep yourself into tunnel vision. If an interview isn't going the way you anticipated, dump that approach and try another. Be ready and willing to change tactics quickly.

Some people like to write questions out in advance. Personally, I feel this practice makes interviews too mechanical and closes you off from other potentially important avenues of inquiry. Still, it might be a good idea to note the main topics you want to cover—you don't want to forget anything. But always be prepared to abandon them if something promising turns up. Don't be surprised if you have to discard all your plans and preparation. And, if the situation calls for it, don't hesitate to scrap it all.

Consider the Interview Location

People will respond differently in different environments. Before the interview you need to decide the best place to conduct it. Here are a few of the more common sites, and some of the advantages and disadvantages of each.

- *The subject's home.* This is the most common location and, in my opinion, usually the best. As long as you take care that you're not seen as an invader, the subject will feel most at ease in his own territory. This can, of course, backfire. In some cases, a relaxed and confident subject will either resent your intrusion, or could feel comfortable enough to lie to you more readily.
- *The subject's place of employment.* Very few people want a detective to show up where they work. They don't want their coworkers or employers to wonder about them. This option tends to elicit either of two extreme responses. The subject may refuse to talk with you (or simply give you a shallow, unsatisfactory interview). Or he may tell you everything you want to know without the usual song and dance, just because he's in a hurry to get you to leave.
- *The detective's office.* This is good for more formal interviews. An office tends to make people more serious. The subject is more likely to tell you the things he thinks you ought to know. Conversely, he is likely to leave out details he may consider extraneous—details that may, in fact, be of vital importance.

- *A neutral arena.* On occasion, it might be best to meet a subject at a restaurant or bar. I've done interviews in parks, beside swimming pools, and in public libraries. A neutral arena is usually the best choice for a subject who is cooperative, but wants to remain anonymous—the neighbor of a philandering husband, for example, or a witness in a personal injury suit against the witness's employer.

Preparation can't guarantee a good interview any more than a good interview can guarantee you'll get good facts. But being properly prepared will certainly increase the chances of getting a good interview. And that's reason enough.

Getting In the Door

Why on earth would anybody willingly let a detective into their house? Unless the detective is working for you, there is no way to know what he's up to. He has his own agenda. To let such a person into your own home, to let him ask detailed, intimate questions, seems an act of madness. Yet, as I said earlier, most interviews take place at the home of the person being interviewed. Why *would* anybody let a detective into their home?

I'll tell you why. Because detectives make people *want* to let them in. Or make them think that they that they should, or must, let them in. They manufacture a reason for being let in, shape the reason to fit the situation and the individual, then sell it.

Here's how it's done:

- *Preparation.* I keep repeating this, I know. I repeat it because it's so important. Before knocking on any door, the detective knows something about the person behind it. Even if he couldn't check out the person prior to the interview, he knows something. It might only be his knowledge of the neighborhood, or his impression of the house, or the toys scattered in the yard. It might only be his intuitive awareness of human behavior. But he knows *something*, and he builds on that knowledge and uses it.

- *Pay attention to details.* Also repeated; also important. Seemingly minor details can help you tailor your presentation to fit the situation and the person. Whenever you enter the home of a subject, give it a quick but thorough examination.
- *Smile.* It's harder to refuse a smiling face. There are, of course, times when it's inappropriate to display a smile. I was once unlucky enough to show up at the home of a witness about twenty minutes after the family had returned from the funeral of the man's wife. My eager, smiling face was totally out of place.
- *Stress your need.* The term *need* is more powerful than *want.* "I need to ask you a few questions." "I need a few minutes of your time." People are usually more responsive to need than to want.
- *Be ready to improvise.* You only have ten to fifteen seconds to evaluate the subject and decide whether to use, modify, or discard the approach you had tentatively decided on.

I once worked a drug case in which the police had discovered a quantity of drugs in a locker located in the cellar of a man's apartment. The defense attorney wanted me to look at the cellar and find out who had access to it and to the locker.

Unfortunately, the defendant had moved out of the apartment after the arrest and it had been re-rented. I knew nothing about the new tenant—I didn't know the person's name, age, history, or even gender. Nothing. But

I knew the kinds of people who tended to live in that neighborhood, which was in a fairly high crime area. I knew the people who lived in the neighborhood were generally poor, suspicious and resentful of authority, and familiar with hard times.

Armed with only that minimal knowledge, I knocked on the door of the apartment. I had hoped a man would answer. It would be easier to talk a man into letting me—a total stranger—snoop around in his cellar. Instead, a young, attractive woman opened the door. The door opened into the kitchen, where a small television was playing. The woman had apparently been reading *TV Guide*, because she held it in one hand with her finger marking her place. In the background, I could hear several children playing.

So, in the few seconds since the door was opened, my fund of information about the new tenant was dramatically increased. Very little of the information was directly helpful, but every bit of knowledge helps. It was unfortunate that the new tenant was a woman. (Women tend to be more cautious than men.) To make matters worse, she was a very attractive young woman. (It's been my experience that attractive women tend to be more suspicious.) And there were children in the house. (Women with children are *very* protective.) Since she was too young to be the mother of that many children, I assumed she was babysitting for working mothers. A young, attractive mother with a house full of children. It could only have been made worse if she was pregnant and confined to a wheel chair.

It was the television in the kitchen and the *TV Guide* in the woman's hand that I counted on. People who have a television in the kitchen watch a *lot* of television. And a lot of television shows are about police and detectives. And I was, after all, a detective. It was almost like an invitation.

I gave her a smile and introduced myself. As in all criminal cases, I identified myself. But instead of giving her a business card, which is my normal custom, I showed her my private detective license. Once she realized my reason for being there had nothing to do with her, that I only wanted to inspect her cellar, she asked me in.

The rest was easy. She asked me questions about the job, and I told her a few lies to make it sound more interesting. Then she gave me a guided tour of the cellar. The information I discovered down there, by the way, was instrumental in winning the case.

Although the key in this situation was unusual (being a private detective hampers more often than helps), it illustrates the need to pay attention to details and to use those details to improvise new tactics. The best approach to a man who answers the door in a T-shirt that declares "They can take my gun when they pry it from my cold, dead fingers" will be different from that of a woman whose bookshelf contains the complete works of Andrea Dworkin.

Pay attention, pay attention, pay attention.

BASIC INTERVIEWING TECHNIQUES

After all the forethought and planning, after you've managed to get in the door, you still have a lot of work to do. You still have to find out what that person knows.

There are no absolutely correct techniques for interviewing. Everybody has his own style, forged from his own unique set of life experiences. But these styles are usually based on the following standard interviewing practices:

1. Develop a rapport with the subject.
2. Ask the proper kind of question.
3. Maintain control of the interview.

These basic practices form the foundation on which individual styles are built. It's like any craft; once you master the basics the rest will come. Michelangelo probably started out sketching stick figures.

Develop a Rapport with the Subject

Easy to say, but somewhat more difficult to do. Those details I keep advising you to pay attention to will give you clues to help you develop a rapport. For example, if a man has the head of a moose over his mantle, choke back any animal rights sentiments you may have and compliment him on the trophy. Ask him about the type of weapon and ammunition he used to slay the beast. Admire his skill at stalking the beast, even if you know that a moose is only slightly more wily than a Guernsey cow.

You're there for information, not to proselytize.

Ask the Proper Kind of Question

At the beginning of an interview, it is usually best to ask general questions (such as "What happened?"), then let the subject answer at his own pace and in his own words. Once you have the general outline of the events, you can begin to ask more specific questions.

There are two basic question forms: closed questions and open-ended questions. Each has advantages and disadvantages.

- Closed questions are those which can be answered with a single word or a short, precise answer: "Who was there?" "What time was it?" "Did you see a weapon?" Yes or no. Up or down. Black or white.

Closed questions have the advantage of being simple and specific. However, they restrict the subject's response. A simple yes or no response rarely provides the detailed information you want.

- Open-ended questions are more general and free-flowing: "What did you see?" "Who was there?" "What did you feel?" They elicit a greater amount of information than closed questions. But they require more time, they allow the subject to cover irrelevant material, and they demand more participation by the subject.

Just as there are types of questions you *should* ask, there are also types you should avoid.

- *Avoid leading questions.* Leading questions taint the answer by supplying information to the subject. "Jones was there, wasn't he?" "Did you notice that the woman was wearing glasses?" These are particularly dangerous questions when asked of children, who are more suggestible than adults.
- *Avoid double-barreled questions.* These are actually two questions rather than one. "Was he drunk or doing anything unusual?" "Did you go to a doctor or mention it to anybody?" You can never be sure which part of the question is being answered.
- *Avoid questions that presume information.* It's easy to make assumptions about things that haven't actually been stated. "Does he prefer cocaine to heroin?" "What sorts of venereal diseases has he had?" "How many times a week does he get drunk?' You may have heard from other witnesses that the subject gets drunk every weekend, but until that particular witness says that the subject drinks to excess, the question shouldn't be asked.

Maintain Control of the Interview

An interview is delicate. To do it well requires a firm but subtle touch. Given the chance, some subjects will talk for hours and not answer a single question. This may be unintentional. Or it may be quite deliberate. In either event, you have to exert a certain amount of control.

Early in the interview, while you're still developing a rapport and getting a general feel for the subject, you may want to let them discuss what may appear to be irrelevant topics. Indeed, early in the interview, you're not always certain what *is* relevant. But don't let yourself get sidetracked. Keep your purpose firmly in mind at all times.

Whenever possible, talk to the subject privately. The more people present during an interview, the less control you have. If the interview is at the subject's home, try to do it in a separate room. Or on the porch, or in your car. If the interview is in a bar, try to move to a quiet spot, away from the subject's friends.

I once had to interview some bikers in a stabbing case. I found them in the bar where the stabbing had occurred. They refused to talk to me one at a time, or even to leave the bar to sit at a table. *Faggots*, I was told, sit at a table; *men* stand at the bar. It only took a short while before I lost all control over the interview. The bikers, who had taken somewhat more drink than was good for them, began to argue among themselves about what had taken place the night of the stabbing. A fight nearly broke out and another stabbing was averted only by the bartender's threat to ban the bikers from the bar if the police had to be called again.

Controlling the interview allows you to set the pace and the tone of the interview. You can speed it up when it gets bogged down in trivialities; you can slow it down if important details are being skimmed over too lightly.

Some Subtle Points

Once you're familiar with the basic interviewing techniques, you can begin to refine them. Here are some of the more subtle points to consider.

Use language familiar to the subject. Try to speak at the same level as your subject. Not in the same style, necessarily (nothing sounds sillier than a white guy trying to talk "street black"), but at the same social level. Talk like a banker to a banker, like a dock worker to a dock worker. But *only* if you can do it naturally. People can tell if it's not natural, and they won't have any respect for you. There are exceptions, as always. If, for example, you want to intimidate the subject, start out talking at an equal social level then switch to a different level. Formal language can sometimes frighten a biker more than a tire iron, and a sudden switch to the construction worker level can show an accountant that you mean business.

Know when to use silence. Silence during an interview almost always works to the detective's advantage. If it stems from the witness giving thought to a matter, it usually pays to stay quiet. If, on the other hand, the silence is a product of the witness's reluctance to talk, it still pays to keep quiet. An awkward silence makes the witness uncomfortable. In his attempt to fill the silence, he's likely to say something revealing. Remember, if it's awkward for you, it's agonizing to him. Wait him out.

Know when to use embarrassment. Normally, when people see somebody embarrassed, they try to make him feel better. And when people are embarrassed, they usually try to hide it. You can use this to your advantage. I once had an assault case in which a woman had allegedly been hit by a man she'd met at a bar. I went to the bar where the incident took place to interview the waitress who had waited on them. Understandably, the waitress wasn't being very cooperative. While I was there, one of those freaks of chance took place: the woman who was the alleged victim came in and ordered a beer. Before she could drink it, however, another patron spoke to her and pointed to me—apparently telling her I was there asking questions about the incident. The woman walked over to where I was talking to the waitress, threw her beer at me, then left. I was humiliated, but instead of trying to hide it, I let the waitress see it. She gave me a bar towel and took me to a back room. Partly as an apology and partly in an effort to explain the woman's behavior, she talked about the events of the night in question, in the process of which she answered all the questions she'd avoided earlier.

Know when to be rude. There are times when good manners just get in the way. If, for example, the subject is blatantly lying or deliberately avoiding a question, you may want to shock him back into line. It requires a delicate touch, but an occasional demand to "cut the shit" can be effective.

Know when (and when not) to appear stupid. It's rarely a good idea to let your subject know how much you know. Some situations require you to seem as dumb as a box of rocks. If people think you are stupid, they may let information slip out unintentionally. Or they may explain things in greater detail so even an idiot like you can understand. On the other hand, it sometimes pays to act as if you already possess all the information you need and just want it confirmed. If people think there is no point in hiding information, they might tell you everything.

Interviewing Mistakes

Most critical interviewing mistakes come from underes-
timating the subjects—not as information sources, but
as people. Too many detectives allow themselves to feel
superior to their subjects. After all, *we* have the secret
knowledge; *we* see the larger picture; *we* know everybody's role.

Wise up. Even the most dull-witted person can sense
emotional dishonesty and can resent it. And that can
ruin your interview.

Here are a few suggestions to help you avoid some of
the critical mistakes in interviewing:

- *Never tell a lie that isn't true.* In an effort to establish
  a rapport, I am sometimes less than totally honest
  with the person I'm interviewing. In fact, at times I
  lie through my teeth. I invent family members with
  problems similar to those of the subject; I develop
  ailments like the subject's; I like or dislike the same
  sports teams; I prefer the same make of car or truck;
  I like or hate the same people. But, when I say these
  things, they're not lies. I *believe* them. I don't understand it, and it's probably an indication of a serious
  personality disorder, but when I say such things,
  they seem *true* to me. I can't tell you how to do it, but
  I strongly advise you never to tell a lie that isn't true.
  People can sense counterfeit emotion.
- *Never let your own opinions intrude.* Your convic-
  tions are irrelevant. If you are an ardent Socialist
  interviewing a staunch Republican, keep your views
  to yourself. You can debate on your own time. Do
  the job.
- *Never think of another question while one is being
  answered.* This is a common error and it can be a

grievous one. Treat each question as if it is the only one you get to ask. And then pay attention to the answer.

- *Never judge.* As the poet said, "We're all bozos on this bus." Nobody likes to feel they're being judged.

Triggering Recall

People forget things. Important things like telephone numbers and names and anniversaries and birthdays and where they put the car keys. To expect people to have a detailed recollection of an event that might have taken place several months or years ago before requires a leap of faith that would make Aquinas himself tremble. And if that event was emotionally traumatic, the difficulty in recalling clearly is compounded.

Forgotten, however, doesn't necessarily mean gone forever. You've probably experienced the frustration of *almost* remembering something. The harder you tried to remember, the more the memory seemed to elude you. Then later, while you were relaxed and thinking of something else, that memory leaked out like water from your ear after a day spent swimming at the beach.

With proper questioning, you can induce that experience in others. A person's memory can be refreshed and a wealth of information can be obtained, information the subject thought he'd forgotten.

You *must*, however, be very careful not to plant information in the subject. While you should encourage recollection, you shouldn't prompt it. And you certainly shouldn't invent it (or help the subject to do so).

There are a number of methods for jogging a person's memory. These are the ones I've found most productive. Remember, these are simply guidelines that you can, and should, modify to suit your own style and needs.

1. *Establish a specific reference point.* Find something that the subject recalls clearly and work from that. The reference point could be the time an event took place, or the persons who were present at the incident, or what the subject was wearing at the time it happened. Begin with general criteria, then become more specific. Did the incident take place before or after Thanksgiving? Did it happen before or after the evening news?

2. *Cover the incident in reverse chronological order.* Most people tell stories in a straightforward chronological order. First X happened, then Y, and then Z. After the subject has given his initial account of the events, ask him to tell it backwards. Before Z happened, Y took place, and that was just after X.

3. *Have the subject consider the incident from a second perspective.* Naturally, people tend to report what they see from a single perspective. Anything else would lead us to question the subject's mental state. However, when asked, people can usually adopt the point of view of any person present when the incident took place. Or even a person not present—an imaginary person. Having the subject relate the events from a new perspective can produce information the subject had forgotten.

These techniques aren't foolproof. Nothing is. But they work. And remember, they're simply guidelines for you to build on.

Body Language

I was talking to a young man who claimed to have seen my client attack a buddy of his outside a bar and stab him a couple of times with a broken beer bottle. The attack, according to the man and the alleged victim, was unprovoked. The client claimed he couldn't recall the fight—he was in an alcoholic blackout.

We were sitting on the porch at the home of the witness's grandmother. He sat in a rocking chair; I was perched on a porch rail. As we talked about the participants in the fight, or about the fight itself, the man rocked quietly and slowly in his chair. But each time I asked specific questions about the events leading up to the incident, he would stop rocking.

We went through the story twice. After the second rendition, I stared at him for a moment, then shook my head and sighed audibly. I slid off the porch rail, put my hand on the back of the rocker and, in a quiet voice, asked him why he was trying to run a load of bullshit by me.

It was, of course, the rocking—or the lack of it—that gave it away. The man finally admitted his buddy had instigated the fight and had, in fact, impaled himself on the broken bottle while rushing to grapple with my client.

We're all familiar with the concept of body language. We all know that people give subtle, unconscious signals that others interpret almost subliminally. We all know it's there, and we all pay some small attention to it. We just don't analyze it.

But you *can* study and analyze it. Body language isn't unique to humans. Animal behaviorists spend a lot of time cataloging animal body language—the appeasement gestures of wolves, the bluffing behavior of pachyderms, the mating signals of the great apes.

Human body language is subject to the same methods

of study. In fact, if you read some primatological stud-
ies, you'll see an uncanny similarity between ape body
language and our own. Watch the posturing that takes
place in a singles bar on a Saturday night and you'll
notice that people aren't much more subtle than apes.
Fortunately, most people don't pick lice off each other
and eat them. Not in the bars I frequent, at any rate.

Body language is, I'm afraid, too complex to cover in
any detail here. Entire books have been devoted to the
subject and for a complete study of the issue, I would
advise you to buy one.

Nonetheless, there are a few things you need to keep in
mind. There are primarily two facets to body language:

> • Interpretation—reading the body language of
>   others.
> • Subliminal communication—sending body
>   language messages.

A good detective needs to be able to do both.

Interpretation. In order to correctly decipher a person's
body language, you should pay close attention to your
subject's eyes, hands, feet, and general body posture.
These tend to be the most expressive and reliable body
messengers, and should receive most of your scrutiny.

> • *Eyes.* I don't know about eyes being windows to the
>   soul, but they're usually good for a peek into a per-
>   son's emotions. A person who refuses to meet your
>   gaze *may* be lying. On the other hand, a person who
>   stares you down may also be lying. At the risk of
>   sounding corny, a person who constantly shifts his
>   eyes *may* be concealing something. I'm also told that
>   a person's pupils tend to dilate when they are lying.

I've looked for this reaction, but have never seen it. Still, it may be true.

- *Hands.* Drumming fingers could mean anything from impatience or distraction to lying. Pay attention to see how relaxed the subject keeps his hands. I've seen people smiling and laughing as if they didn't have a care in the world, while at the same time they gripped the arms of their chair so hard their knuckles were white.
- *Feet.* Maybe it's because they're so far from the head, but people who seem able to control all their other automatic responses often seem unaware that they are tapping or wiggling their feet and toes. I can recall a man whom I suspected was an accomplice to a burglary assuring me he was concealing nothing from me, while his feet were doing a frantic drum solo.
- *General body posture.* A person's posture can tell you when (or if) he is receptive to an interview or if he is lying, hostile, defensive, frightened, or any of a number of things. Pay attention to contradictory messages, such as an appearance of composure while the subject's palms are sweating. And note exaggerated postures—for example, a person who has been accused of a heinous act who appears absolutely unruffled.

These few suggestions don't even skim the surface of body language. A good detective should note a rapid increase in the subject's breathing, or a tightness of the jaw muscles, or any indication that all is not as it appears.

There are a couple more things you'd be wise to remember. First is that nothing happens in a vacuum. Each detail you note *must* be examined as part of the whole. If your subject is wiggling his foot, it could indicate that he is nervous, or distracted, or impatient. Or

perhaps he has an illness that affects his motor coordination. Or it could simply mean that his bladder is full.

The second thing to remember is that body language
only gives you limited understanding. It's useless as a
method for trying to comprehend motives. You may be
able to tell that a subject is lying to you, but you still don't
know *why* he's lying. And you don't know what the truth is.

Finally, it's important to remember that different cultures have different body signals. In our society a refusal
to look someone in the eye is suspect; in some cultures
looking a stranger in the eye is considered offensive.
Don't expect a person born in Thailand to have the same
body signals as a person born in Tulsa.

Subliminal communication. There are times when the
ability to send subliminal messages is as important as
being able to interpret them. Take, for example, what
you do with your hands. Sticking them carelessly in
your pockets shows the person you're with that you trust
them, that you don't feel the need to protect yourself.
Jamming them in your pockets, however, can indicate
that you're concealing something, such as agitation or
nervousness. Hooking your thumbs in your pockets is
somewhat more forward than actually sticking your
hands in your pockets. Indeed, it is sometimes interpreted as sexually aggressive. What you say by putting
your hands open on your hips is different from what you
say by resting your fists on your hips.

Consider the "power stance" police officers commonly use—hands on hips, feet apart, militarily erect, preferably looking down at you, their body slightly invading
your personal space. That pose is no accident; police
officers do it deliberately to intimidate the person
they're talking to. And it works.

So be aware of your own body language. Think about

what you want your body to say. Although it's usually in the detective's best interest to appear harmless, there might be occasions when you want to adopt a power stance or to put on a display of impudence.

Whatever message you send by body language, be certain you're doing it deliberately.

An awareness of body language should also include an awareness of interpersonal space and territoriality. Most Americans feel comfortable having an impersonal conversation with a person about three feet away. If you move closer, subjects subliminally feel you have invaded their personal space. They get a little tense, a little uncomfortable, though they don't always know why.

The same concept applies to territoriality. If you sit at a table with another person, you will both tend to automatically divide the table between you. This is my half, that's yours. If you move things onto the other person's half of the table, again, they get tense and uncomfortable without understanding why.

You can use these subconscious reactions to your advantage. If, for some reason, you want your subject to be distracted or uneasy during the interview, invade his personal space. A slight invasion is usually enough. Indeed, moving too close can provoke a violent reaction.

Verbal seduction works. It gets you in the door. It gets people to talk to you. It helps you to control the pace and the direction of an interview. It dusts off the old memories stuck in the cobwebbed corners of the mind. It allows you to interpret the nonverbal messages sent to you, and guides you in the messages you want to send.

It really works. If you pay attention.

When most of us think of the law, we think of the police, dramatic courtroom scenes, and hard-eyed criminals. In fact, only a small portion of the law deals with crime. Most legal battles take place in the arena of civil law.

Civil law is the law of common crises. It deals with the problems we all encounter—people falling in and out of love, people having accidents, people being negligent or careless, people arguing over the possession of property, people running away from each other.

A detective can help find out who did what, where, and with whom. Knowing these things can sometimes help determine who gets what when it's all over.

Much of what a detective would do, you can do. By being your own detective, you can save yourself some time, some trouble, maybe some heartbreak, and some cash.

R.G.

Chapter 8

CIVIL WORK

A wife suspects her husband of having an affair; a wrench dropped by a careless construction worker hits a man on the head as he's walking through an unmarked construction site; a sixteen-year-old girl has an argument with her parents and runs away from home; a divorced mother worries that her children aren't receiving proper care during the weekends they spend with their father.

These aren't cataclysmic events. They're the simple, common tragedies of modern life. Sadly, they're also the source of much of a private detective's income. It's called civil work—civil as opposed to criminal work. Civility, I'm afraid, has little to do with it.

Civil work may not be the stuff dreams are made of, but it *is* the stuff bills are paid by. Civil work is meat and potatoes to most detectives. It's the most commonly requested type of detective work. It's no coincidence that civil work is also the most lucrative investigative field.

In civil work, no crimes are being committed (or at least nobody is being charged). There aren't necessarily any villains involved. It may even be that nobody is at fault. Civil work revolves around the frailties of people, people who are just trying their best to cope with tough times.

Sometimes people need a little help. They want to know if their husbands are having affairs; they want to sue the construction company for hospital costs; they want to find their children; they want to make sure their children are safe. But they don't know how to find out about those things.

So they call on private detectives.

Although civil work is a diverse field, most of the work can be divided into three categories:

- Domestic
- Missing persons
- Personal injury

There is also a great deal of insurance work out there. Insurance work, however, largely consists of surveillance and tailing, which are covered elsewhere.

DOMESTIC

Things fall apart, as the poet Yeats said. He wasn't talking about marriage, or whatever arrangement people use in place of marriage, but his observation is still appropriate. Things do fall apart, sometimes despite a person's best efforts to keep them together. The domestic fabric unravels.

Private detectives get involved before, during, and after the unraveling. These are the three most common matters for domestic investigation:

- Marital infidelity
- Divorce litigation
- Child custody

They aren't pleasant matters. If they were, there wouldn't be any need for a private detective. Nobody calls on a detective unless they're stuck in something potentially ugly.

Marital Infidelity

People trash around. They have affairs, one night stands. They shack up for long, illicit weekends. Men, women— it makes no difference. Infidelity is an equal opportunity transgression.

This isn't based on any research, but men seem to trash around more than women. That could just be a difference in the degree of access to willing partners. As women enter the workforce in larger numbers, there seems to be a concomitant increase in trashing around. Women seem to be better at it, though, if you consider being harder to catch to be better. Men are notoriously stupid.

Men also tend to be more consistently vindictive when they suspect their wives or lovers of having an affair. They want motel doors kicked in and compromising photographs taken. They want their unfaithful partners punished and humiliated. Their pride is hurt.

Women, on the other hand, usually want information. Who is she? Why her? What does she have that I don't have? Why is this happening? But it's been my experience that if a woman *does* become vindictive, she usually makes male animosity seem pale in comparison.

I confess, I've never kicked in a door of any sort, motel or otherwise. (Well, I did once; but it was to stop a suicide attempt, which doesn't really count.) I *have* taken a few compromising photographs. But mostly what I've done is watch and pay attention. And I try to teach the client to do the same.

There are a number of things a person can do to determine if their spouse or lover is trashing around:

1. *Pay attention to any marked change in sexual appetite.* A sudden decrease or increase in sexual appetite could be symptomatic. A

person's sex drive might decrease due to
guilt, or simple exhaustion. An increase in
appetite could be an attempt to cover up, an
over-reaction in an effort to show that nothing is wrong. Or it could reflect a bolstered
self-concept. An affair can make a person
feel more attractive to the opposite sex.
That new awareness can boost a person's
interest in sex. When you feel seductive, you
behave in a seductive way.

2. *Note any marked change in mood.*
Irritability, sudden and unusual generosity,
bursts of anger or weeping. For most people, having and hiding a long-term affair is
emotionally taxing. The strain usually
shows in one way or another.

3. *Keep track of the odometer readings on the
partner's car.* Unless they travel as part of
their job, people tend to drive approximately
the same number of miles every day. To the
office and back, for example, or to school
and to the market. In contrast, people having
affairs usually prefer to have them away
from a neighborhood where they might run
into people they know. The miles can add up.

4. *Search the partner's pockets or purse.* Look
for telephone numbers and matchbooks.
Check for receipts for hotels or flowers.
People having affairs are often very senti-
mental and will keep "souvenirs" of their
trysts. I know a man who kept the key to
the hotel room where he met his lover.
Room 2102, as I recall.

5. *Check all credit card receipts, automatic teller
slips, and cancelled checks.* People having
affairs, and especially men, tend to buy gifts

for their lovers. Also check for receipts for gas stations in a part of town the partner rarely visits.

6. *Examine the partner's clothing.* Look for hair that obviously doesn't belong. Check for unusual smells, such as perfume or cigarette smoke.

7. *Critically examine the reasons for your suspicion.* Don't jump to conclusions. Pay attention.

8. *Consider asking the lover or spouse.* It's amazing how often people will talk about their suspicions to anybody but the person who matters most.

I realize the suggestions listed above may be offensive. Searching the clothes of a loved one is certainly a violation of trust. So is infidelity. I only make the suggestions. You—or the partner involved—have to wrestle with the moral decision of whether or not to follow the suggestions.

There was a woman who suspected her husband of having an affair. Once or twice a week for a couple of months, he'd been late coming home from the office. He'd claimed he'd had to work late, but on a couple of occasions she'd tried to reach him at his office only to learn he wasn't there. He'd also been moody, she said, and emotionally withdrawn. She didn't want to confront her husband about the matter; she just wanted to know if her suspicions were well founded.

The woman followed the suggestions listed above. She noticed that on the nights her husband "worked late," the odometer read a few more miles than normal. She'd also found a credit card receipt for flowers on the floorboard of their car.

With that information, I began tailing the man home after work. On the third day, he led me to a cemetery.

Cemeteries are ideal places to check for a tail. There isn't a lot of traffic, which makes it easier to spot a tail. Larger cemeteries often have multiple entrances, so a person doesn't have to leave the same way he entered. They're also good places to meet someone you don't want to be seen with.

I couldn't tail the man into the cemetery for fear of getting burned, so I parked my car and walked in. It was a large cemetery, and I gave up after half an hour, assuming he'd left by one of the other gates. I drove to the client's home and set up a surveillance on the house. The husband arrived about forty minutes later.

Twice more in the next ten days I tailed him to the cemetery. Each time I hurried to another entrance hoping to catch him. Each time I failed. I decided I would have to advise the client that we needed to hire more help to guard the other entrances to the cemetery.

As I worked on other matters during the day, I kept wondering about the husband. The cemetery routine was clever. Where did he learn it? Was he being extraordinarily cautious, or had he spotted me that first night? There was nothing in his history to suggest he might know anything about losing a tail. Maybe it was a coincidence. Maybe he was just taking a short cut. Maybe.

Then it occurred to me—cemeteries have a purpose other than as a device for losing tails. They bury dead people there. A little research (and the judicious application of a fifty-dollar bill) gave me the names of everybody who'd been buried in that cemetery since the husband had started "working late."

One of the names was familiar. It was the same last name as the husband's. A visit to the city hall revealed that the person was the husband's father.

I spent the next three days staking out the father's grave. On the third day, the husband drove up near the marker and stopped. He didn't get out; he just spent the next forty-five minutes sitting in his car, smoking. Then he drove away.

I reported this to the client. Her husband hadn't mentioned to her that his father had died. She told me her husband rarely spoke about his father—an alcoholic who had routinely beaten his wife and children. Despite all the evidence, the husband wasn't having an affair; he was exorcising some personal demons.

The point of that story isn't that you can't rely on circumstantial evidence, but that evidence can often have more than one interpretation.

Divorce litigation

The beginnings and endings of all human undertakings are untidy. That's what the English dramatist John Galsworthy said, and I've seen very little to dispute it, especially where marriage is concerned. The beginnings may be fine, but the endings of relationships can be untidy indeed.

Some marriages simply dissolve. No fuss, no bitterness, no animosity. The people involved seem genuinely sorry things didn't work out. Other marriages explode in flames and consume everybody involved, and sometimes innocent bystanders as well.

When a marriage explodes, people get weird. People who are normally pleasant turn into creatures that would make werewolves shy away. People who are usually kind, thoughtful, and considerate develop a sadistic streak that would make Torquemada cringe.

Although I have been around the block a few times, I'm still regularly shocked—and often frightened—at the pure, malignant spite of a former loved one.

I've seen couples at each other's throats over a Boston fern, or a collection of mystery novels. During one bitterly contested divorce, I was hired to track down a dog.

The couple involved in the divorce, thankfully, had no children. But they were disputing custody of the family dog, a Japanese breed called an Akita. They'd actually litigated the issue in court, and the husband had been granted temporary custody of the dog pending the final settlement.

A few weeks later, the dog disappeared from the yard of the house the husband was renting. The man assumed his soon-to-be-ex-wife had snatched it. He wanted me to prove it (not to see if it was true, but to *prove* it) as ammunition for the divorce. He was more interested in getting his ex-wife in trouble than in the welfare of the poor dog. I agreed to look into it.

It only took a few hours to determine the ex-wife didn't have the dog at their house. Later that evening I followed her to her boyfriend's apartment and shifted the tail to him. I wasted the next few days tooling around after the man, watching him drive to work, shop for a new tie, and buy Chinese take-out.

But on the weekend, he and the ex-wife-to-be went to visit friends in the country. The dog was there, of course, looking healthy and happy and content.

I reported it to the client. That was my job, after all. But I refused his request to fetch the dog back. I figured the dog was better off out there. No reason the dog should suffer because its owners were acting like beasts.

A lot of private detectives refuse divorce work. Not because it isn't lucrative, but because it can get so nasty. Given the option, I'd always choose a nice, clean murder or arson over divorce work. Crime is so much less depressing.

Most divorce work consists of digging up dirt on the other partner. This is usually done by means of tailing and surveillance, by rummaging through the trash, and by interviewing friends and neighbors. All of these techniques are covered elsewhere in this book.

Child custody

This is one of the most distressing and disheartening facets of detective work. In disputes over child custody, one parent normally accuses the other of being unfit to care for their children. This usually involves an accusation that the other parent is neglecting, or actually causing harm to, their children.

Sometimes the accusation is a ploy in a vicious divorce proceeding. Sometimes it's just another punishment technique by the person who feels the most injured by the divorce. Sometimes it's true. There's no way to know until the facts have been critically examined.

There are a number of methods for investigating child custody matters. But remember, a good detective never sets out to *prove* anything. A detective just gathers and examines the facts.

1. *Interview neighbors.* Neighbors, if properly approached, can provide a lot of information. People develop a feel for their neighbors. They overhear arguments, they notice the hours their neighbors keep, they hear children cry. During the interview you should stress that knowing such things doesn't mean a neighbor is nosy. Information of that sort is acquired unconsciously.
2. *Interview teachers and friends of the children.* Children sometimes talk to their teachers; they almost always talk to their friends (who sometimes relay that information to their own parents). Teachers may also notice changes in behavior that might reflect on the quality of the care the children are receiving. A shift in a child's grades

can be important. When interviewing the friends of children, be certain to get permission from the friend's parents. Parents can get hostile if they discover their children have been interviewed without their knowledge or permission.

3. *Interview the children themselves.* If possible, make every effort to interview the children separately and alone. The presence of either parent could affect the child's responses. Watch for signs that the children have been coached by either parent.

4. *Surreptitiously photograph the children.* A candid shot of unkempt children going to school can be very telling.

5. *Examine the trash.* Check to see what sort of food the children are eating. Make special note of grocery receipts. The trash can also reveal if a parent is drinking too much.

6. *Be objective.* There are usually alternative explanations for most things. Don't read more into the situation than what is actually there. It's an investigation, not an inquisition.

Child custody matters are trying. But it is critical that they be examined carefully and in a professional manner.

MISSING PERSONS

The term "missing person" is often a misnomer; for the most part, these people aren't missing. They didn't just get lost, they've run away. Wives leave their husbands. Husbands desert their wives. Children flee from their parents, and parents abandon their children. The reasons may vary, but the result is the same. Somebody who matters is gone, and somebody who is concerned (or sometimes merely angry) wants that person found.

People who deliberately run away are usually more difficult to locate than strangers who simply aren't where they are expected to be. But, by paying attention and exercising a little patience, it can usually be done.

The difficulty in finding a runaway, regardless of the subject's age, is a factor of how seriously that person planned his or her escape. Most people don't plan very far in advance. Some sort of precipitating event happens, they see it as the last straw, they decide they've had enough, and they leave. If the person is an adult, they *might* prepare a few days in advance, but usually not.

The techniques for searching for runaway juveniles and adults are essentially the same as for locating strangers (see Chapter 6). The locations searched, however, tend to be drastically different.

Juveniles

Kids run away for different reasons than adults. The reasons, oddly enough, are less important with kids. What is critical with juvenile runaways is the severity of the crisis that provoked the departure. And you can't always tell how severe the crisis is from the precipitating event. A kid might be prompted to run away after his parents refuse to let him watch *Psycho VIII*. The kid may see that refusal as part of a long, restrictive pattern. That crisis might be more severe than that of another child who runs away after being punished for wrecking the family car.

When looking for a runaway child or teen, always carry a recent photograph of the subject and show it frequently. Here are some suggested steps to consider when juveniles disappear:

1. *Check with the youngster's friends.* Don't expect too much at first. Friends will usually protect each other. At least for a while. Eventually, however, the romance of it wears off and they are more likely to talk. Also be certain to talk to the parents of the friends. They may notice that junior is spending more time than usual with another buddy, which could establish a pattern of the support network for the runaway. They may also be aware of increased spending on their child's part. Again, check the trash. Kids have a strong need to keep in touch with each other. Look for post cards, letters, and notes passed in school.

2. *Check at the school.* Teachers are rarely much help in runaway cases, but it's often useful to conduct a surveillance of the school beginning about forty-five minutes before classes end for the day. School, even for those who hate it, is the place to meet friends.

3. *Check malls, video arcades, and fast-food restaurants near the school or the homes of friends.* Kids often hang out in such places. They also learn how to cadge food and spare change there.

4. *Check the youth shelters in the nearest major city.* These shelters are often sponsored by religious groups. They tend to be very cooperative as long as you aren't too demanding. Leave a photograph with them.

5. *Check bus depots.* Not just in your town, but in the nearest city. Kids are much more likely to travel by bus than any other mode of transportation. It's cheaper, and, for a lot of kids, has a sort of gritty romance to it.

Obviously, if a youngster takes a car, report it as stolen, even if the car belongs to the kid. What harm can it do?

Adults

When adults leave, they're usually more serious about it than juveniles. They're more likely to have a plan. Even so, their plan is usually to go somewhere else and start over. Very few people go through the bother of getting false papers, assuming they even know how. For the most part, they don't become different people, they just become the same person in a different place.

They usually eat at the same types of restaurants, maintain the same hobbies, subscribe to the same magazines, follow the same sports. I know a detective who found a missing husband by waiting for basketball season to begin. The man, who had abandoned his wife and children in the late spring, was a passionate Celtics fan. He hadn't missed a weekend game at Boston Garden in twelve years. The detective went to the first weekend game of the season and, sure enough, there was the man in his usual seat. He'd moved from a suburb of Boston to a small town on the coast near Cape Cod. But he hadn't been able to give up his seats. Do you know how hard it is to get decent tickets for Celtics games? The hardest part of the job, according to the detective, was scrounging a ticket for himself in order to get in the arena.

As with juveniles, it's a good idea to keep a fairly recent photograph handy during the search. Here are a few suggestions:

1. *Check with friends.* Especially *old* friends, like old college roommates or army buddies.
   Again, examine their trash for telephone calls, return addresses on envelopes, and so on.

2. *Check with family members.* It's difficult for most people to totally abandon their family. There's a good chance that a runaway will stay in touch with at least one family member, although that person will probably be reluctant to talk about it. Be certain to examine family trash after birthdays and holidays (especially Mother's Day) for card envelopes with return addresses and for telephone bills. Also, interview the neighbors of the subject's parents. People like to talk about their children, even after they've grown up.

3. *Check the last place of employment.* People usually give their last job as a reference for their new job. Find out if the previous employer received any such calls. If possible, get the names of companies that do similar work and companies that the subject was in regular contact with. Check them out. If the subject had a Rolodex at his place of employment, try to get a look at it. Business contacts are valuable; people hate to lose them.

4. *Check schools.* It's not uncommon for women, when they run away, to go back to school, even on a part-time basis. In order to be accepted by any college, the subject must supply other school transcripts. Check with the registrar at any school the subject attended before running away.

5. *Check with the subject's union.* Some occupations are limited to union members. Since people tend to take similar jobs, and since a union card often guarantees higher wages, many union members will maintain their membership. If the subject was a union member, check with his local. Although I

hesitate to advise you to be dishonest, you
may want to lie to them. Tell them he hasn't
picked up his last check and you need his
new address in order to mail it to him.

Oddly enough, timing plays an important role in tracking down missing persons. People who are missing for
either a short amount of time, or for a very long period
of time, are more difficult to track down. A runaway who
has been gone a few months is easiest. When people have
been gone long enough to settle into their new lives,
they've also been gone long enough to start missing old
friends and family. At that point, they get careless and
make mistakes. And that makes them easier to find.

Of course, not all missing persons have run away to
start new lives. Sadly, some have run away from life
itself—they have killed themselves. Others, those with
deteriorated mental states, just get lost and wander off.
A few, mostly children, are kidnapped.

The bodies of the suicides usually turn up eventually,
and most of those who wander off are located by the
police. People who are suicidal tend to seek out low
spots, cellars or valleys in the woods. Those who are lost
often do the opposite; they seek the high ground, as if
looking for direction. Those who are kidnapped are
rarely heard from again.

Not very pleasant, perhaps, but you knew life wasn't
all beer and skittles.

PERSONAL INJURY

An elderly woman waited at the curb for the light to
change, then began to slowly and carefully cross the
street. She'd only taken a few steps when she heard
sirens. Looking up, she saw the flashing lights of an

ambulance—just before it hit her. The ambulance knocked the woman down, breaking her hip and arm.

As a result of her injuries, the woman faced huge hospital bills. Having only a meager fixed income, she was hoping the ambulance company would help pay the bills. She hired a lawyer to see if she had any hope of getting a settlement from the ambulance company. I was hired by the woman's attorney to find and interview witnesses to the accident.

The woman didn't personally blame the ambulance company for the accident. She assumed the drivers were involved in an emergency, and she admitted she hadn't moved out of their way. She felt the accident was essentially her own fault. But she needed some help with the hospital bills and felt the ambulance company would be her best bet. She wasn't a crook; she was just broke. The lawyer accepted the case on a contingency basis; he would only get paid if a settlement was reached.

I interviewed a lot of witnesses, all telling essentially the same story. They had heard the sirens; they saw the flashing lights; the old woman made a gesture as if she was going to move out of the way, but didn't. Some felt the ambulance driver didn't try hard enough to avoid hitting her. Others felt the driver had made a heroic effort to avoid her. But they all agreed on one unusual fact. Although a second ambulance arrived to treat the old woman and transport her to the hospital, nobody had seen the patient in the first ambulance. No third ambulance arrived to transport the patient, and nobody saw the patient transferred from the first ambulance to the second. Perhaps the patient had expired on route and there was no longer any need to rush. At any rate, after the police had been on the scene for an hour or so, the first ambulance simply drove away.

Out of curiosity, I began to check on the patient in the ambulance. Both the hospital and the ambulance company refused to cooperate. But after a little research, I discovered where the ambulance had been coming from at the time of the accident.

A heavyset man, after eating a big meal, had experienced chest pains and shortness of breath. He thought he was having a heart attack, and his wife called the ambulance. When it turned out to be nothing more serious than heartburn, the man was treated at the scene and the ambulance crew left. The wife said she overheard one of the ambulance crew say that he was going to be late for a date.

And that, it turned out, was the case. We learned during a deposition of the ambulance crew that the driver had used his sirens and flashing lights to avoid traffic because he was late for a date. There was no patient in the ambulance. There was no emergency. According to one of the crew, the driver was glancing at his watch when he struck the old woman.

A lot of people get injured through no fault of their own. The toaster explodes, or they slip on a newly washed floor, or they get whacked by an ambulance driver with a hot date. They did nothing wrong, yet they suffered an injury. Somebody has to be held accountable.

When such an event happens, the victim often decides to bring a suit against the people responsible. A lawyer handles the legal issues, and a detective gathers the evidence. Here are some of the ways to go about gathering that evidence:

1. *Decide who is to be sued.* In the case mentioned above, the decision was made to sue the company as well as the driver. The company, after all, had trained the man, and the man was acting as an agent of that company at the time of the accident. Besides, the company had more money than the driver.

2. *Visit the site.* This should be done as soon as possible after the incident, because things are likely to change afterward.

I worked on a case where a man, in a hurry to visit his wife in the hospital, had taken a short cut through an area where a new wing was being added. There were no warning signs, no notice not to use the sidewalk through the area. The man had stepped in soft cement and in the resulting fall had torn ligaments in his knee. The very next day, the area had been roped off and was littered with warning notices.

If the incident took place in a public spot, the visit should be made at the same approximate time as when the incident took place. That will allow you to see scene conditions most like those experienced by the victim. It also gives you the opportunity to find people who may have been witnesses.

3. *Take photographs.* Again, this should be done as soon as possible after the incident. Photograph the scene, photograph any injuries suffered by the client, photograph everything. Take lots of photographs. Film is cheap.

4. *Talk to witnesses.* This is obvious, isn't it?

5. *Get written statements.* Again, as quickly as possible after the incident. People forget things, so if possible, have the witness write out the statement. But go over the information first and ensure that it is in logical order. If the witness is reluctant to write the statement, write it for him, one line at a time. And check each line with him. Get it right the first time. You may not get a second chance.

With personal injury, the operative word is *personal*. The people involved are often injured in more than a merely physical sense. The old woman who got whacked by the ambulance was made to feel frail and weak. She lost confidence in her ability to take care of herself. Even though she recovered physically, she was never the same woman emotionally.

In a way, that's the essence of civil investigative work. These are the simple, common tragedies of modern life. And while they may not be tribulations on a grand scale, they're devastating to the people involved in them. Sometimes it's difficult to remember that the measure of a tragedy is how the people involved are affected.

My client swore he wasn't guilty. Nothing new.

This one was a grandfather, a kindly, white-haired old man who said he had no idea why his stepson's nine-year-old daughter was saying he'd touched her where he shouldn't. He loved her, my client said, just as if she was his own granddaughter. He showed me her picture. She was cute, with blue eyes and blond hair in pigtails and a spray of freckles across her nose. My client told me how smart she was, how she read books, and that she was the smallest child in her class. He just loved her, and he couldn't understand. He was humiliated because his name was in the newspaper; he was too ashamed to go to the local market. And he was afraid of what was going to happen. He cried in my office.

He swore he was innocent, but since the child stuck to her story, we went to trial.

When she testified, she had to sit on telephone books in order to see the jury. She said Grandpa had given her milk and cookies and afterward had made her stand still while he put his hand under her dress. She said she was scared and looked out the kitchen window. She said she watched the neighbor's kittens playing and watched the clouds floating by and tried to think of what they were shaped like. She said she was embarrassed and didn't tell anybody what had happened. Not until a few weeks later when another girl at her school told a teacher that she had been touched by her grandfather.

Greg and I went to the client's house. We looked at the kitchen window. There was only one, over the sink. All you could see was the shoe factory next door. No sky, no clouds. The neighbor had no kittens, nor did anybody on the block remember ever seeing kittens.

Was she telling the truth about everything else? I don't know. My client said she wasn't. Was she trying to get the same sort of attention the other girl in her class got? I don't know.

Reasonable doubt. That's all it takes.

R.G.

Chapter 9

CRIMINAL WORK

Television, once again, has it all wrong. When they aren't skidding around corners and seducing beautiful women (or being seduced by them), TV detectives spend their time solving crimes and catching crooks. When they help somebody accused of a crime, their client is always innocent.

In real life, detectives are rarely involved in catching crooks. Operatives who work for big security firms might be in hot pursuit of embezzlers and pilferers, but for the most part catching crooks is done by police officers. That's what we pay them for, and they usually do a pretty good job.

In this chapter, we're going to examine the private detective's role in the criminal justice system. You'll learn what really happens and why it happens that way. I'll give you a short course in criminal defense techniques. By the end of the chapter, you'll see that the criminal justice system is not a world of clarity but a hazy, smoky world in which it isn't always easy to tell the good guys from the bad.

Private detectives doing criminal work normally work for a defense attorney. Criminal defense work is usually considered the least attractive field of the detective business. Typically, it is less lucrative, the pressures are more intense, the risks are higher, the working conditions are worse, and the rewards fewer. And the client is almost always guilty.

Before we examine the techniques and strategies of criminal defense work, we need to address an ethical question: If you know your client is guilty, how can you possibly defend him?

You may not find the ethical answers entirely satisfactory. Get used to disappointment. So very few answers *are* entirely satisfactory.

Imagine a client, a middle-aged man accused of sexually assaulting a twelve-year-old boy. The police also suspect him of kidnaping, raping, and possibly murdering a number of other young boys. He's already served a prison term for a similar crime.

The man is absolutely guilty of the crime he is charged with. He has admitted it to you. You believe he is guilty of the other crimes as well. All of them.

The man is a loathsome, despicable creature and a very real danger to society. Nobody in their right mind would want such a person free to roam the streets. Why should you defend him?

For the following reasons:

1. The police make mistakes.
2. Sometimes the police prevaricate.
3. Everybody is presumed to be innocent until proven otherwise.
4. The threat to individual civil liberties is more compelling than the danger to individual safety.

There are, of course, other reasons. Everybody who does criminal defense work has his own unique reasons. But those are the most common ones. Let's examine them more closely.

The Police Make Mistakes

Not often, but it happens. We've all heard of people released after years of imprisonment following the discovery of evidence showing them to be innocent. With the advent of DNA testing, this seems to be happening more frequently.

You need to understand something about police procedures, something they don't like to advertise. The police solve crimes in much the same way that doctors diagnose diseases. Doctors see a set of symptoms and, based on their knowledge and experience with disease, they associate those symptoms with certain specific diseases. They perform a few tests to help them sort out which particular disease is responsible for an illness. Then, based on the results of those tests, they treat the patient for that disease.

The police see the results of a crime and, based on their previous experience and knowledge of the local criminals, they associate that type of crime with certain known criminals. They perform some tests (fingerprints, witness interviews, and the like) to help them sort out which particular criminal is responsible for the crime. Then they build a case against that person.

They're usually right. Usually. When the police decide who they believe committed the crime, they focus on that person to the exclusion of all others and construct a case against him. It's the most efficient way of doing it.

But what about the few times when the police are wrong? They're still convinced of the person's guilt. That's why they arrest people. They just happen to be mistaken on occasion.

We simply cannot count on the police to catch and correct their own mistakes. The framers of the Constitution realized that, which is one of the reasons they gave the prosecution the burden of proving beyond a reasonable doubt that a person accused of a crime actually committed that crime.

Sometimes the Police Prevaricate

The term *prevaricate* sounds more pleasant than *lie*. But call it what you will, on occasion, the police will bend the truth. They usually feel they have good reasons for lying. Sometimes they *know* a person is guilty of a crime, they know with absolute and mathematical certainty, but they can't prove it. It has to be frustrating.

So they stretch the truth. Not really with the intention of deceiving the court, but with the hope of making the community safer. Their intentions are almost always good.

But we all know good intentions aren't enough. That police officers tell lies is bad in itself, but sometimes it is especially wrong. See "The Police Make Mistakes."

I knew a man who had been arrested more than a dozen times for driving without a license. But each time the man went to court, something happened. The police or the prosecutor botched some part of the case, or a witness failed to appear, or the documents certifying the man's license had been revoked got lost in the mail. Although there wasn't the slightest doubt the man had committed those crimes, something always happened and he always got off. The police were disappointed and understandably livid.

Then a police officer, one who had personally arrested the man on four prior occasions, claimed to see him driving again. The officer was off duty at the time, and in his own vehicle, so he didn't give chase. But he noted the time, the make and model of the car, and the location. He swore in an affidavit that he clearly saw the man driving, and a warrant was issued for the man's arrest.

At the trial the officer again swore under oath that he had clearly seen the man driving a car. He was quite forceful about it, and the defense attorney could not get him to admit he may have been mistaken. Then the defense put on its witnesses. They included several of the town councilmen, who testified that at the time the man was allegedly driving he was actually attending a town meeting. Over a dozen witnesses, all upstanding citizens, saw him there.

Not only was the man acquitted, but the judge who issued the arrest warrant refused to ever again accept that police officer's sworn word. The officer eventually had to resign and find work in another town.

He wasn't a bad cop, normally. He was just frustrated at what he saw as a miscarriage of justice. So he tried to correct it. But you can't enforce one law by breaking another.

Everybody Is Presumed Innocent Until Proven Guilty

The presumption of innocence is one of the foundations of our criminal justice system. In our adversary system, the prosecution has most of the advantages; they have legions of trained police officers, detectives, forensics experts, photographers, and pathologists at their disposal. All the defendant has is a lawyer and, if he is lucky, an investigator. The presumption of innocence and the prosecution's burden of proof are meant to help balance the scale.

If the prosecution weren't required to prove the guilt of every single defendant in every single trial, then it would become easier to convict the few people who actually are innocent. It doesn't matter how blatantly guilty the accused is, the prosecution must always be forced to prove his guilt.

The Threat to Civil Liberties

Sir William Blackstone, the British jurist, said it was better for ten guilty persons to go free than for one innocent person to be wrongly imprisoned. Every time a person accused of a crime is placed on trial, our legal system is on trial with him. If the law doesn't protect everybody, then nobody is safe from the danger of being wrongly convicted.

When a guilty person is set free, some part of the community is placed at risk. But when an innocent person is imprisoned, the foundation of our society is placed at risk. That's the greater danger.

What about the rights of the victim? Obviously, the rights of the victim were violated. That's what brings the issue to the public forum of a trial. Unfortunately, a right that's been violated can't be fully mended. It can't be retroactively protected. That applies to the victim as much as to the accused. It's the responsibility of the government to mend the violation by ensuring that the guilty person is brought to trial and *legally* convicted. But the focus at the trial stage must shift to the defendant's rights; those rights can still be protected. Two wrongs don't make a right, as my mother used to tell me.

That's what justifies defending a person like the child molester I mentioned earlier, even though it's not possible to defend what he actually did. It isn't always pleasant. But it's very important.

So much for the ethics. Now for the practical question. How is it done?

There is an old criminal defense aphorism: If the facts are against you, bang on the law. If the law is against you, bang on the facts. If both the law and the facts are against you, bang on the table.

The attorney does the banging, but it is often the detective who provides the hammer.

Understand this: The defense team is not on a quest for The Truth. That's the prosecution's job. The defense is only required to protect the rights of the accused and to ensure that the prosecution follows the letter and intent of the law.

The techniques used in criminal defense investigation are basically the same as those used in other investigative work. The only difference is the direction in which those techniques are focused.

What follows is a quick introduction to criminal defense work. It is by no means comprehensive. It's just a quick and dirty look at the way things are done.

There are two primary methods for defending a client accused of a crime:

- Attack the prosecution's case.
- Build your own case.

Each tactic has its advantages and disadvantages. In some cases they can be combined effectively.

ATTACKING THE PROSECUTION'S CASE

Attacks on the prosecution's case can be made in many ways. The following three methods of attack are the most common:

- *Demonstrate that the prosecution's witnesses are confused or unreliable.* Cast doubt on their credibility or honesty. Provide witnesses who can refute prosecution witnesses. This does not mean the defense can smear or slander the witness. But if there is any evidence that the witness may not be trustworthy, the jury has the right to know it.
- *Show that the manner in which the evidence was col-*

lected, processed, or stored was improper. A lot of physical evidence is easily tainted or damaged. If proper procedures weren't followed, then the evidence may be unreliable. This could involve anything from the failure to place bloody clothing in a paper bag (bloody cloth sealed in plastic will rot) to making certain that a proper chain of evidence was followed. (A piece of evidence that can't be accounted for, even briefly, is suspect because it may have been tampered with.)

- *Offer proof that the prosecution acted illegally.* Any evidence that the police obtained in willful violation of the law must be excluded. Any evidence falsely manufactured or altered by the police must be excluded. There is a legal concept referred to as "the fruit of the poisonous tree." The underlying idea is that fruit which comes from a poisonous tree is tainted and should be discarded. Evidence obtained in violation of the law is also tainted and should also be discarded.

I was involved in an arson case in which the defendant was accused of starting a fire in an apartment building. An old man died in the blaze. Our defense was that the fire had actually been a result of faulty wiring, and that the fire had been smoldering for several hours before the time our client was alleged to have set it. A few days after the fire, we examined the entire building—every apartment, floor to ceiling. We took hundreds of photographs, we walked on balconies barely supported by their charred beams, we ruined our clothes crawling through the rubble. We worked our way through the burned out structure like ants. And we found plenty of evidence to support our theory.

Then, on the day of the trial, the prosecutor showed us some newly developed photographs of the interior of the building. Visible in each of the photographs, which had been taken in various apartments throughout the building, were clocks. Wall clocks, oven clocks, even clocks in the bathroom. The clocks had all stopped at the same approximate time—and it was the time the police claimed our client started the fire.

We were devastated. Our entire defense had been destroyed by those pictures. All that work for nothing.

Then we looked at our own photographs, the ones taken just a few days after the fire. Many of the same clocks shown in the police photographs were also visible in ours. But they were all stopped at a different time than the clocks in the police photos.

Somebody had altered the hands of the clocks. At some point after we'd inspected the building, somebody had entered the sealed building, adjusted the clocks to support the prosecution's case, then resealed the building as he left. (We later discovered it had been done by a member of the fire marshal's office.)

The judge, after he saw the evidence had been tampered with, dismissed the case against our client. You can't break the law to enforce the law.

BUILDING YOUR OWN CASE

As with attacking the prosecution's case, there are several ways in which the defense can build its own case. These are some of the most common:

- Demonstrate that the client was elsewhere when the crime took place and therefore could not have committed the crime. This is an alibi defense. Unfortunately, in the minds of the general public, the term *alibi* has become synonymous with *lie*. In fact, an alibi is simply an assertion that you were somewhere else at the time.

- Show that the crime was, or could have been, committed by somebody other than your client. Remember, the burden of proof is on the prosecution to prove that the accused committed the crime. By demonstrating that the crime may have been committed by another person, the defense establishes reasonable doubt in the minds of a jury.
- Show that no crime was committed. This is often a difficult approach, but not impossible—as demonstrated in the following example.

I once assisted in the defense of a man who had been accused of destroying a small-town police station. The town was so small that only a single police officer was on duty at night. While that officer was out on patrol, somebody stole a bulldozer from a nearby landfill and deliberately drove it into the station. If that wasn't enough, the person then backed up and crashed into it again. The building was destroyed. There were witnesses to the incident who, despite the late hour, were certain they recognized the offender. My client was arrested a short time later.

On the surface, it wasn't a good case for the defense. There were no apparent weaknesses in the prosecution's case. But the prosecution had to prove every element of the crime, which in this case included authorization. They had to show that the accused wasn't authorized to destroy the police station.

By a fluke comment made by a witness, we learned that the property on which the police station had been built was not owned by the town. A little research confirmed that the property was actually owned by a private citizen who had intended to donate the property to the town but had failed to follow through with the paperwork. On top of that, the station had been built with donated materials.

On the day of trial, the authorization matter was brought before the court. The prosecution couldn't produce the owner of the property, so there was nobody who could testify that the client wasn't authorized to destroy the building. Nobody could show that a crime had been committed.

The client walked.

To reiterate, there are two main avenues of criminal defense: attack (the prosecution's case) and build (your own case). Attack and build. Each of those avenues has two components: the law and the facts.

The law is the attorney's responsibility, so I won't devote much time to it. But a criminal defense investigator needs to be familiar with criminal law. Knowing what constitutes a legal arrest or a legal search can help you ask the right questions or recognize an important fact overlooked by the attorney. Lawyers are no less fallible than the rest of us.

The Law

In order to convict a person accused of a crime, the prosecution has to prove that a specific act took place, that the act violated a specific law, and that it was committed by the person accused. If they can't prove those things, the defendant walks.

What does all that mean? Consider a person charged with as simple a crime as drunk driving. The elements of this crime differ from state to state, but we'll generalize here. In order to get a conviction, the state has to prove a total of six different things. They have to prove: (1) operation of a (2) motor vehicle on a (3) public way while (4) the defendant was under the (5) influence of (6) an intoxicant.

Sounds simple, doesn't it? But let's look at those elements more closely:

1. *The vehicle has to be in operation.* This seems clear enough. But what if the guy was found drunk and passed out behind the wheel of a car parked along the side of the road at night with its motor running, the headlights on, and the radio playing? Is he operating the vehicle? What if he's awake, but just sitting there cheerfully drunk in his car? What if the police find the car crashed into a fence, and he's drunk behind the wheel? Can he be charged with operation? How did the car get there if he didn't operate it?

2. *It has to be a motor vehicle.* Again, this sounds obvious. But what if a man gets roaring drunk, rolls a car with no engine out of the garage, and coasts down the hill in it? Is it a motor vehicle? A power boat is a motor vehicle, but what about a sailboat?

3. *The vehicle must be operating on a public way, a space where public traffic may operate.* A private driveway is not a public way, but what if the guy is drunk enough to drive on a sidewalk? Or what if he gets popped while driving on the beach?

4. *It must be proven that it was the defendant who was operating the vehicle.*

5. *The defendant must be under the influence.* Most, if not all, states have set arbitrary blood alcohol limits to determine the degree of intoxication. The standard is a blood alcohol content (BAC) of .10, although in recent years some states have changed their standard to .08 BAC. Some states consider impairment to begin with a .05 BAC. Reality, of course, fails to comply with the legal standard. Some folks will be able to function

normally with a .20 BAC, while others will
be staggering drunk with a .04 BAC.
6. *Finally, the defendant must be under the influence of an intoxicant.* What if the guy has been taking cough medicine? Does that count?

In legal terms, drunk driving is a relatively simple crime. If a case of drunk driving is this convoluted, try to imagine the complexity involved in a rape or homicide.

Again, in addition to proving that a specific act broke a specific law, all the evidence collected by the police has to be legally obtained. This is that fruit of the poisonous tree mentioned earlier. Evidence illegally obtained by the police isn't allowed. There are exceptions, of course. In the law, there are always exceptions.

Obviously, these are just the bare bones of criminal law. The more law you know, the better off you are as a detective.

THE FACTS

Although knowledge of the law is primarily the responsibility of the defense lawyer, the discovery and disclosure of the facts is the detective's job. Facts belong to no one. Facts are out there waiting for whoever asks the right person the right question in the right way. A strange thing about facts is their mutability, the way they change. Ten people seeing the same event often produce ten contrasting sets of facts about the event.

The detective acts as the attorney's eyes and ears. He collects and confirms the information the attorney needs to present the defense. Despite what you see in the movies, attorneys almost never go into the field and discover witnesses and evidence. Even if they wanted to, there is no way they could present that evidence in court. An attorney can't call himself as a witness and testify as to what he saw or learned.

In concept, a defense investigator's job is simple. He merely gathers information. Whether that information helps or hurts the client is, for the investigator, totally irrelevant. The defense attorney needs to know the bad facts as well as the good in order to be prepared for the prosecution's case.

In reality, the job is anything but simple. It is often alarmingly complex. But it can be made easier if you follow some simple guidelines.

Talk to Everybody Involved

The victim's version of the facts will rarely agree with that of the person accused. Does that mean that one of them is lying? Probably. But not necessarily. Each witness has a different perspective on what took place. Talk to as many of them as possible. Pay attention to what they say. Every inconsistency in their stories helps the defense.

I was involved in the defense of a man charged with knifing another guy in a bar brawl. It was a bar for bikers (motorcycles, not bicycles) and the clientele was known for being rowdy. There had been twenty people or so in the bar when the fight broke out. I interviewed as many as I could find in the time I had.

About a third of the bikers said my client started the fight; another third said the fight was provoked by the victim. The other third refused to talk to me.

At the trial, the prosecution put on all the witnesses who claimed the fight was started by the defendant; the defense, naturally, put on the others. Of the fourteen witnesses who testified that they saw the fight, none could agree on all the facts. The jury was left with the impression that none of the witnesses really knew what the hell had happened—which was probably true.

Limit Your Assumptions

It would be best if you could assume nothing, but that isn't realistic, so try to be stingy with your assumptions. For example, it would be a mistake to assume that your client is always telling you the truth. Or that the police always include all the facts in their reports.

I worked on a case where a police officer, after stopping a car, saw what he believed to be stolen property in the passenger seat of the car. The reason he stopped the car, according to his report, was because the driver was swerving as he drove. And that was true, the driver *was* swerving. What the officer failed to mention, however, was that the road was under construction and full of pot holes. Everybody swerved on that section of the road.

A judge found that the police officer had no legal reason to stop the man. The stop, therefore, was illegal. Any evidence found as a result of the illegal stop was chucked out the window. The case was dropped.

The more assumptions you make, the fewer questions you ask, and that increases the odds that you'll miss some crucial piece of information.

Examine the Physical Evidence

Defense teams too often accept the prosecution's interpretation of the physical evidence—the bloody clothes, the twisted remains of the car, the detritus of crime. This is often because the defense doesn't have the money to have the physical evidence tested by independent experts. The prosecution's interpretation is usually correct, it's true. But not always.

For example, I had a client who was charged with torching a car. The car was set on fire in the parking lot of a body shop just down the street from a convenience store. The crime took place during the early hours of the morning. The police and fire department responded to the scene, and the fire was extinguished. Both the police and the fire fighters stayed at the scene for a period of time after the fire had been put out.

The following day, the police found two candy-bar wrappers in the front seat of the car. They interviewed the people who lived and worked near the scene of the fire, including the people at the convenience store. A clerk told them she'd sold a couple of candy bars to a man shortly before the fire was noticed. The man was a frequent customer and she knew his name. Unfortunately, she couldn't recall what type of candy bar he'd purchased.

The man, who was a well-known troublemaker, was questioned. When it was discovered he had a grudge against the owner of the car, he was arrested and charged with arson.

By the time I got the case and had a chance to examine the car, it had been hauled behind the auto body shop. The seats were burned and the heat had been intense enough to melt the dashboard. The entire interior of the car was coated with thick, black, greasy smoke.

I wasn't going to bother driving to the police station to look at the candy-bar wrappers. How much information could be gleaned from a pair of burnt and smoke-covered candy-bar wrappers? But the attorney insisted. After all, the candy-bar wrappers were the only physical evidence (as opposed to testimony, or verbal evidence) linking the client to the arson. To appease her, I went. And it was a good thing I did. The wrappers weren't burned, nor were they covered with smoke. They were just crumpled candy-bar wrappers.

How could those wrappers escape the heat, which was capable of actually *melting* the dashboard? How could they avoid the greasy smoke that covered everything else in the car? How?

They couldn't. A visit to the convenience store clerk revealed that some of the fire fighters had purchased sodas and chips after the fire was extinguished—and a few candy bars.

Did the wrappers found in the car come from the fire fighters? Or from the defendant? I don't know. Neither did the jury.

The client walked.

View the Scene of the Crime

This seems obvious, but it is often overlooked. And for good reason; the scene rarely provides any helpful information. But when it does, it's usually a big boost for the defense. Juries love to look at the scene of the crime. It gets them out of the courtroom, it gives them a chance to wander around town when everybody else is at work, it makes them feel more involved.

I had a client who was accused of possessing drugs with the intent to distribute them. The client was known on the streets, and by the police, as a drug dealer. I'd been involved with the same client in an earlier drug case, which the prosecution lost when it was revealed the police had obtained their evidence illegally. The police were not amused by the result. They were upset enough that the case had been dismissed; the fact that the dismissal was a result of their own mistakes made the matter worse. Who could blame them for being upset?

But they were more than upset. They were angry and vengeful and determined to try again. It had become personal. They wanted that person behind bars. Somehow.

And, at first glance, their second attempt looked solid. The drugs were found, according to all reports, in a locker in the cellar of the defendant's apartment.

Most of my investigation centered on the client's alibi, which was shaky at best. It wasn't until a few days before the trial that I went to the apartment where the drugs were found. The apartment had been re-rented, but I managed to talk my way in and get the new tenant to show me the cellar.

The cellar, it turned out, was shared by three other tenants. Each tenant had a separate door leading into the cellar. In addition, there was an outside bulkhead door with a broken lock. Anybody could have entered that cellar.

There was no way to establish with certainty who put the drugs in that locker. None of the tenants, including the client, claimed ownership of the locker. Nor could the contents of the locker be traced to any of the tenants.

The jury walked through the cellar, and shortly thereafter, the client walked out of jail.

There you have it—criminal defense investigation in a nutshell. Attack and build, law and fact. That gives us a matrix of four potential defense strategies:

1. Attack based on the facts.
2. Build based on the facts.
3. Attack based on the law.
4. Build based on the law.

That's the way it's done.

In most of the cases I've mentioned in this chapter, the defendant was freed. That's not an accurate portrayal of real-life defense work. In real life, most of the clients are guilty and most of them plead guilty or get convicted. And the green grass grows all around, all around.

In many ways our justice system has little to do with justice. Our courts are *not* courts of justice; they're courts of procedure. The procedure is designed to remove the jangled and stretched emotions of the events that brought all the parties to court, to allow a calmer and more reasoned evaluation of those events. Although they appear to be bent to benefit the guilty, the procedures are really there to protect the innocent.

It's been my experience that despite its flaws, despite its inadequacies and apparent inequities, the system actually works. It's slow and sometimes aggravating. But it works. And it works *because* of the procedures, not despite them.

I knew a bailiff at one of the courthouses, a former police officer whose knee had been shattered in the line of duty. He was a man who had witnessed a great deal of pain and suffering during his career, a man who had experienced pain and suffering himself. As he'd grown older, he'd grown more tolerant of the frailties and weaknesses of others. I was talking with him one afternoon while waiting for a jury to finish its deliberations. It was one of those pathetic cases in which everybody involved—the defendant, the witnesses, the victim—was guilty of something, and everybody was a victim in some way. As we discussed the people involved in the case, the bailiff told me he was a great believer in compassion and mercy. But justice, he said, kept happening to people. One way or another, people tended to get what they deserved.

Before you set foot on the street, before you start your car, before you do anything discussed in this book, read this chapter. This is for your own good.

Ruth Greenberg has given me a lot of good advice over the years. Most of it legal, some of it personal. But all of it was direct and to the point.

Once, when I was being badgered by a cop and on the verge of losing my temper, she touched me on the arm and said, "Don't do anything stupid." That's good advice for almost any situation. I listened to her and calmed down.

You should listen to Ruth as well. She knows what she's talking about. She's a damned fine lawyer and doesn't couch her advice in a lot of legal language. She tells you right out. She's kept me out of a lot of trouble. And she can do the same for you.

Breaking the law is stupid 99.99 percent of the time. I have, on occasion, stretched the limits of the law. I've even broken it a few times. But I've never broken a law by accident. And I've never done it lightly. The few times I've violated the letter of the law, I knew what I was doing. I weighed the risk against the potential gain, made a decision, and was prepared to accept the consequences.

But each time, I was right on the edge of stupidity.

Listen to Ruth. Don't do anything stupid. If she says not to do something, then don't do it.

G.F.

Chapter 10

THE AMATEUR DETECTIVE AND THE COMMANDMENTS OF LAW

I t would be almost easy to be your own detective if you could do anything you wanted. Torture, deep interrogation, wiretapping, and secret agents are all popular and efficient investigative tools in many countries. Police detectives in those countries have an easy job.

But "a policeman's job is easy only in a police state" (*People* v. *Spinelli* 35 N.Y. 2nd 77, 81–2). Here in the United States, the Constitution and the law limit what the police can do in their investigations.

You, too, must play by the rules. Here are some guidelines for what you, when you are acting as a detective, may and may not do under the law.

These words to the wise cannot include everything that is forbidden. Use your judgment. If you have doubts about your judgment, consult a law library or ask a lawyer. If you still have doubts, ask your mother.

YOU'RE NOT A PROFESSIONAL

You're an amateur. You can do this for love; you can do it for honor; you can do it for fun. But you *can't* do it for money, or in exchange for what lawyers call "consideration" unless you have a license.

Consideration means something of value, a good or a service given to you in return for your detective work. A

Porsche, for example, is goods. You may not accept a Porsche in return for your detective work. A ride in a Porsche is a service. You may not accept a ride in a Porsche in return for your detective work. You may not accept *any* consideration for being a detective unless you have a detective's license. Each state has its own rules about what you need to do to be licensed and you need to follow the rules. This is a regulated industry.

Think of it this way: Although you're not a dentist you can use a pair of rusty pliers to pull every tooth in your own mouth, and you're within the law. If your kinder-garten-aged child has a wobbly tooth, you can pull it. But woe betide you if you set up a sign on your front lawn that says "Extractions—One Dollar." That's illegal.

You can no more conduct an investigation for a con-sideration than you can extract teeth for a considera-tion.

YOU'RE NOT A COP

In the movies, detectives carry guns and shoot people. Usually, they shoot the bad guys, so nobody gets upset.

This is not the movies. Don't carry a weapon unless you have a license and the law of your state permits you to carry it. Check to make sure. Don't shoot anyone, even if he is a bad guy. And don't meddle with criminals. It's not your job. You could get hurt, or you could hurt somebody else, or you could get in the way of law enforcement officials who are trying to do their job.

Getting in the way of law enforcement officers is called obstructing justice, and it's a crime. You may feel the law enforcement people are incompetent and don't know what they are doing. You might, in fact, be able to do it better. But interfering will certainly not make them happy. It might make them unhappy enough to arrest you. Even in the movies well meaning, smart private detectives get arrested. Don't get in the way; it's against the law.

YOU'RE NOT JAMES BOND

Unlike 007, you're not licensed to break the law. You may not commit crimes in the exercise of your detective work. For instance:

Don't Trespass

You can't go onto private property unless you have what lawyers call "license and privilege." While it's certainly easier to look in a person's window if you stand on his lawn, unless you have his permission to stand on the lawn, you're guilty of a crime. That's why it's called private property. In most states, you can go to jail for trespassing. Find some other way to get the information.

Lest you get too discouraged, remember that much property is jointly owned. Many people can give permission to enter it. In many apartment houses, you don't need permission to be in entryways, in halls, or on the roof. In many buildings, the landlord can authorize permission to enter specific apartments, and the tenants need never know. And, of course, anybody who actually lives in a residence can authorize you to enter—spouses, children, or grandparents.

But if it's private property, and you have no permission to enter, keep off. There's very little information worth going to jail for.

Don't Destroy Property

Greg mentions an incident in which he broke the tail-light of a truck in order to make it easier to follow. He broke more than the taillight that night; he broke the law. Good detectives often tread a fine line. But they are paid to take risks, and the good ones always weigh the costs and benefits of their actions.

You are not licensed to destroy anything, even a tail-light. Depending on the value of what you destroy, you could go to jail for a while. Courts don't look kindly on those who take the law into their own hands. So don't do anything stupid.

Don't Do Drugs

You many want to remain alert while conducting a lengthy surveillance. Eat sugar, drink coffee, slap your-self—but don't take any illegal drugs. There is no excep-tion to the laws against amphetamine use, not even for weary detectives. If love is not enough to keep you going, go home.

Don't Lie to the Government

Depending on the circumstances, it's a misdemeanor or a felony to give false statements to agents of the gov-ernment. This includes members of the local police department.

This rule encompasses lies written and unwritten, sworn and unsworn. Generally, you are not allowed to give a false name for the purpose of perpetrating a fraud. You cannot deceive with the intent of obstructing justice. It is rarely a defense to such a charge that you believe in a different and better kind of justice, or higher law, or even that you were being your own detective.

On the other hand, in most circumstances, you don't have to answer any questions. And unless a police officer tells you that you must stay where you are, you're free to leave. You can refuse consent to be searched, though you may be searched regardless.

But if you elect to speak to an agent of the law, be sure you speak the truth. Or at least avoid telling lies.

Jurisprudence in this area is very complex. For your safety, prudence is the best jurisprudence. Remember these two simple rules: (1) you have a right to remain silent, and (2) it's wrong to tell a lie.

If you *are* questioned by a police officer, you can always ask for a lawyer. Once you ask for a lawyer, the officer isn't supposed to question you further. He might, but he'll probably pause a moment to consider the situation. That will give you a moment to think as well. Still, it's wiser to think first.

YOU'RE NOT A PEST

You cannot harass people. You have a right to privacy, and so does every other private citizen.

Harassment is a legal term of art; you can be sued for it and you can be convicted of it, but nobody can tell you exactly what it is or how close you can go to the edge without dropping off the deep end.

Professional detectives sometimes work close to the edge. That's their job. But they're bonded and insured just in case. You aren't. So I suggest you follow this very conservative legal advice. If a person says he doesn't want to talk to you, leave. If a person tells you to get off his property, leave. If a person catches you following him, leave.

If these things happen to you with any frequency, however, you should re-read the book. You're doing it wrong.

YOU'RE NOT AN ADVOCATE

A detective's job is to *find* the facts, not to create them or alter them to fit a desired pattern. Here are two rules to keep you within the law:

Don't Tamper with Witnesses

Be careful not to influence a witness to change his story. It isn't that difficult to do. It can be done, for instance, by threatening to kill, injure, or shame him. Or you could offer him money or maybe a trip to Cleveland (threat or inducement, you decide). Getting people to change their story is illegal and could earn you a long time behind bars.

You can also change people's stories accidentally. For instance, if you repeat to one witness what another witness said, you may taint the first witness's recollection beyond repair.

A good detective lets each person tell his story.

Don't Touch Any Evidence

If you suspect that something is evidence of a crime, leave it alone. Don't touch it. Don't hide it. Don't move it. Leave it alone. You're in way over your head, and you could be committing a crime—obstructing justice or aiding and abetting.

You don't have a legal duty to turn evidence in, or report it to anyone. But disturbing evidence of a crime may ruin material that the police, if they found it, could use. So don't touch it! Don't even touch anything near it!

Those are the only exclamation points you'll find in this book. They're there for a good reason. You can't afford to play in a game with stakes that high.

YOU'RE NOT A BUS

A bus is obliged to pick up every person who wants a ride, as long as that person has the fare. Buses are considered common carriers and must give service to anyone who asks.

A detective is not a bus. You can pick and choose the people you work for. Just because you know how to find things out doesn't mean you have to. You're under no obligation to use your skills, which leads us to the most important rule:

YOU'RE NOT THE SPHINX

Many people think that they have an absolute right to remain silent. This is not true.

If you're being questioned by a police officer or an agent of the State (except in very rare circumstances beyond the scope and focus of this book), you *do* have the right to remain silent. Ask for a lawyer and see the rule about James Bond.

But if you have witnessed something, or heard something, or found out about something, then a judge, in a courtroom, can compel you to tell what you know. At that point, you have the right to remain silent *only* if what you say may tend to incriminate you. For instance, if you happen to learn a friend was hiding a stolen tractor in his garage, you are under no legal obligation to report it to the police. If the police come and ask you questions about the tractor, you don't have to answer them (although you still can't lie to them).

But if you're summoned to court because your friend is being tried for receiving stolen property, the judge could make you testify about what you know. Even if it breaks your heart and the bonds of friendship.

Again, in front of a judge you only have the right to remain silent if what you say might incriminate you. You don't own what you know. You are the mere custodian of fact.

The only thing that keeps you from having to tell is if you don't know. Act accordingly. Consult a lawyer if you have questions. And don't do anything stupid.

Technology lets us get more done, and get it done quickly. It can also get us in more trouble and get us in trouble more quickly. The technology that Greg discusses is available on the open market. It is perfectly legal to buy it, own it and use it. But some of the technology can easily be used to violate the law. There are legal limits to the ways in which you can use some of these devices—and the laws regarding technology change often and vary widely.

The law involving electronic eavesdropping, for example, varies from state to state. Some states require the consent of only one party to record a conversation. Other states require the consent of all parties involved. Similarly, you can use night vision devices to study the behavior of nocturnal animals, but you are not allowed to spy on people where they have a reasonable expectation of privacy.

Check the law before you use these technological advances in your investigation. Stop and look before you listen. Being your own detective does not grant you permission to commit a crime. If you disregard the law, you can end up in jail, where the only thing you'll have to listen to are other inmates.

R.G.

Chapter 11

GOING HIGH TECH

L et's face it, this is the age of technology. It's virtually impossible for most Americans—most humans, in fact—to go through the day without encountering a computer chip. Our cars talk to us, our coffeemakers anticipate when we will wake up, our televisions remember our favorite channels, our refrigerators make ice for us and defrost themselves, our telephones not only answer themselves and take messages but also forward our calls to other telephones. Modern technology has dramatically changed the way we live and the way we see the world. And the cutting edge in technology shifts every few months.

Modern technology has also radically changed some aspects of investigation. In this chapter we'll take a look at some of the ways you can use technology to become a more efficient and effective investigator.

Although the vast majority of investigative work is still done the old-fashioned way (a lot of footwork, a lot of talking, a lot of thinking, and a whole lot of patience), technology has allowed us to enhance and expand the scope of our traditional investigative skills—watching, listening, remembering.

Technology lets us watch better. Instead of relying solely on our own fallible eyes, we can now watch from a tremendous distance. We can now watch in extremely low light—even in total darkness. We can now watch while we're not even there.

It lets us listen better, as well. Instead of relying on our limited ears we can now listen from across a football field. We can now listen from a remote site, totally out of sight of the subject. We can now record conversations and listen to them at our convenience.

And technology allows us to remember better. Instead of relying on our own faulty memories we can now use computers to store and analyze information—and to do it quicker and more reliably. We can also use them to access a wide variety of information that was not often available in earlier eras.

As an amateur detective, you don't need access to the cutting edge of investigative technology—even if you could get it (which you can't). But there are still a number of relatively inexpensive devices that will make your work easier and more effective.

EXTENDING YOUR VISION

There is a certain perverse pleasure to be derived from the ability to see without being seen. Morally and ethically, it's often difficult to justify—but even in those instances in which there is some justification, the pleasure remains a guilty one. And that's a good thing, because it's getting easier to do every day.

Here are some of the most common technologies that will allow you to extend the scope of your vision. The devices discussed are readily available to you. That only leaves you with the problem of sorting out the moral and ethical dilemmas.

Binoculars

Binoculars are incredibly handy tools. Almost every detective I know keeps two pairs. A fine pair of binoculars and car binoculars (a beat-up old pair tossed in the back seat). My car binoculars—an old, much-knocked-around set of 10x50s—have probably been used more often for watching birds and wildlife than for surveillance.

I mentioned that my car binoculars are 10x50s. What does that mean? Binoculars are always referred to by simple numerical designations: 7x35, 8x40, 10x50. The numbers refer to the level of magnification and the size of the objective (front) lens respectively. For example, a 7x35 binocular magnifies the object being viewed by seven times. It appears to be seven times nearer to you than it would appear to the naked eye. And the objective lens of a 7x35 binocular is 35 millimeters in diameter. Now, why is the diameter of the front lens important? It determines how much light enters the binocular. The more light the lens gathers, the brighter the image will be. That's important when you're looking at things in low-light situations, like at dusk or in a shady area.

So a 10x50 binocular will magnify the object more and let in more light than a 7x35 binocular. So, why doesn't everybody just use 10x50s? Because, as with everything else in the world, there are trade-offs. Greater magnification and larger objective lenses mean a bigger device. You can find 7x35 binoculars that will fit in your shirt pocket. 10x50s are larger and therefore much more conspicuous to use. They're also heavier—only by a few ounces, perhaps, but when you have to hold the binoculars steady for a long period of time, even a few ounces can make a difference. It's surprising how tired your arms can get after a short period of looking through binoculars.

For general purposes, I prefer 8x40 binoculars. They're

not as popular or as common as either 7x35s or 10x50s, but they make an excellent compromise between magnification, light gathering, and weight. Lately, pocket-sized 10x25 binoculars have become popular. These are terrific binoculars in good light conditions, but as the light begins to fade, they are less useful.

In addition to binoculars, some detectives also use monoculars and spotting scopes. A monocular is essentially half a binocular. Monoculars work on the same principle as binoculars, although they generally tend to be less powerful. Spotting scopes, on the other hand, are generally more powerful than monoculars and binoculars. In fact, they are basically mini-telescopes. Whereas most common binoculars max out with a magnification of 10x, spotting scopes often range from 8x to 40x magnification. Unlike binoculars and monoculars, which are usually hand held, spotting scopes tend to be attached to tripods. Indeed, the extreme level of magnification makes it difficult for them to be held by hand—the smallest wobble becomes extremely exaggerated at higher magnifications. Tripods, of course, are rather conspicuous to use. On the other hand, with greater magnification, you don't have to be quite so close to the subject to watch him.

Long Lenses

Detectives have two things in common with paparazzi: a willingness to disregard the privacy of other people, and a fondness for telephoto lenses. When you're taking pictures of people doing things they don't want you to see, it helps if you can do it from far away. Obviously, if your subject sees you standing nearby with a camera, he'll avoid the behavior you're trying to observe. Or he'll chase you off.

The standard lens that comes with most 35-mm single lens reflex cameras is a 55-mm lens. This gives approximately the same perspective as the human eye. It's not much use for covert surveillance photography. Neither is the most common telephoto lens, the 135-mm. This is fine for shooting portraits, but it doesn't really allow you to get far enough away from the subject.

The telephoto lenses favored by detectives range from 200-mm up to 1800-mm. An 1800-mm lens will allow you to take photographs from about a mile away from the subject. Not much chance of being spotted when you're a mile away. Of course, you need to be about that far from the subject to use an 1800-mm lens. They're rather conspicuous. An 1800-mm lens is about the size of your arm. And all that metal and glass is heavy.

There are other disadvantages to such long lenses, however. The biggest disadvantage is that these long lenses are extremely susceptible to wobble. They can't be hand held; they require the use of a tripod. This is a disadvantage because it requires you to tote around one more piece of equipment and because tripods always take a few seconds to set up and take down—which can be a problem if your subject is restless. Long lenses are heavy; you can't attach them to a camera and attach the camera to a tripod. Either the tripod would tip over or the lens would break. Instead, every quality long lens has a tripod mount built into the body; the lens itself is attached to the tripod and the camera body attaches to the lens.

Another disadvantage is the sheer distance between the camera and the subject. You can't control who or what will come between you and your subject. Even the simple fact that there's a lot of atmosphere between you and the subject makes a difference. There's a lot of crap floating unseen in the air, and a lot of it diffuses light. That means your photograph will be hazy. That haziness will be exacerbated if there's a heat source between the camera and the subject—say, a tar roof or a highway with a lot of traffic. Heat causes the air to move, and that rippling effect shows up in the photograph.

Lenses over 1000-mm are rarely needed. For most purposes a 500-mm lens is long enough. An inexpensive 500-mm lens can be purchased for less than US$500. It may not be the best lens, it may produce images that aren't perfectly crisp around the edges of the frame, but this ain't art. You don't have to produce a perfectly sharp photograph. All you need to be able to do is to identify the subject.

Night Vision Devices

Night vision devices (NVDs) first saw extensive use during the war in Viet Nam. The most common versions of NVDs are referred to as image intensifiers. They work by amplifying existing ambient light, which is the light that's bouncing around in the air. The further light gets from its source (televisions, streetlights, the moon, car lights, house lamps), the more diffuse it becomes. We may not be able to see it, but it's still there. NVDs collect that light and amplify it tens of thousands of times. The result is observed on a small imaging screen, like a miniature television screen inside the NVD. The screen in most NVDs shows a monochromatic image, usually in shades of green, although the better equipment gives black-and-white images. There are color NVDs, but at the moment only the military has access to them.

I should make one thing clear: image intensifier NVDs don't work in absolute darkness. They require *some* ambient light to work. There are devices that allow you to see in total darkness, but they work on an entirely different process (using infrared radiation) and are prohibitively expensive.

One of the side benefits of the collapse of the former

Soviet Union has been the glut of inexpensive Russian-made NVDs. These work well for most purposes, but warranties and repairs are a definite problem. A number of U.S. manufacturers also make affordable NVDs, which are slightly more expensive than those coming from Eastern Europe but easier to repair.

There are four types of NVDs: sights, bi-oculars (*not* binoculars), monoculars, and goggles. You don't need to worry about sights—they're the NVDs that are attached to weapons and are used by snipers in low-light situations. *Bi-ocular* and *monocular* simply refer to whether the NVD has one or two eyepieces. A bi-ocular has two, a monocular has one. A bi-ocular NVD allows the investigator to look at the image with both eyes, which reduces eyestrain. They don't have the magnifying power of binoculars. Goggles are worn on the head. They can be bi-ocular or monocular. NVD goggles have the advantage of leaving your hands free, which allows you to take notes. There are also handy NVDs designed to be attached to still and video cameras.

The prices of NVDs range from US$300 to US$6,000. As the technology becomes more common, the prices will inevitably go down.

Surreptitious Use of Video Technology

Although video technology doesn't actually allow us to see farther, it can allow us to observe and record events that take place while we're not there. This has the effect of allowing us to extend our vision.

In recent years, we've seen investigative technologies modified for home use. The first innovation was the baby monitor, which is a sort of overt bugging device placed in a baby's room. It allows parents to listen to the baby while they are out of the room doing other things.

A more recent innovation has been the "nanny-cam." This is essentially a videotape recorder hidden within an ordinary-looking object—a radio, a clock, a lamp. These devices, which were developed for the private security industry, allow working parents to record the behavior of child care providers while the parents are at the office. When they return from work, they can replay the videotape to see if their child has been well cared for in their absence. Some folks have also used these devices to catch neighbors and landlords suspected of rummaging through their belongings while they're away. Nanny-cams can cost anywhere from a few hundred dollars to a couple of thousand dollars, depending on the quality of the video equipment and the device in which it's hidden. However, they can often be rented from private security or private investigative agencies.

Recently developed computer software programs and miniature cameras have also extended the range of our vision. It's now possible for anybody with a home computer to monitor activities at home in real time while they are sitting in front of their office computer (although employers may object to using office equipment). This technology is relatively inexpensive; the entire package—software and mini-cam—can be purchased for only a few hundred dollars.

Extending Your Hearing

Television has made us a visual society. We want to be able to *watch*. Obviously, we gain more information if we can see as well as hear, but the truth of the matter is that many people are now uncomfortable listening without seeing. They feel like something's missing. However, for investigative purposes, listening alone is often enough—and it's easier. Listening devices tend to be more compact and more easily concealed than vision-enhancing devices.

I'm not going to spend any time discussing wiretaps and bugs.* Occasionally, you'll find an advertisement for cheap versions of these devices in the backs of odd magazines for military enthusiasts, but these devices are virtually worthless. Although it's not available in the United States at the moment, a Japanese firm is manufacturing a device marketed to protective parents concerned that their children are the victims of neighborhood bullies. These are credit-card-sized radio transmitters broadcasting on an ultrahigh frequency (UHF) band. A receiver allows the parents to listen to the children within a radius of about 350 yards. Eavesdropping technology is improving (although I'm not convinced this is a good thing), but for the present, if you feel the situation requires a bug or wiretap, you should seek out the help of a professional investigator.

Still, there are lower-level technologies that can enhance and extend your powers of hearing. The most common of these devices are voice-activated tape recorders.

Voice-Activated Tape Recorders

When I first began in the detective biz, tape recorders were rather bulky. I carried a state-of-the-art, Japanese-made miniature tape recorder. It was about the size and weight of a small brick. Advances in technology have made tape recorders much smaller, much lighter, and much more effective.

---

* A wiretap is exactly what it sounds like—a device that intercepts a transmission carried over a wire or some related form of telecommunication. This includes fax and computer communications as well as voice communications. A bug is a device that transmits sound from one place to another. A bug doesn't rely on telecommunications; it can be planted anywhere.

One of the most useful innovations was the development of voice-activation technology, usually referred to as "vox". Rather than simply turning on the tape recorder and letting it run while recording long periods of silence, voice activation acts as a switch. It only records when there is a sound being made. The sound must be loud enough to trigger the record cycle. The sensitivity of this trigger can, on better recorders, be adjusted. Vox recording is not actually new technology; the tape recordings that proved so damaging to Richard Nixon were made with vox machines. Modern vox technology is more sophisticated and available on very small recorders.

To use a vox recorder as a bug, simply secrete it somewhere in the room in which you want to record. Obviously, it's best to place the device as close as possible to the area where you suspect the conversation (or sounds) will be taking place. With a little creativity, it's often possible to get the recorder very near the action. For example, with a little duct tape, a vox recorder can be attached to the bottom of a coffee table. The cord of a button microphone (which may come with the unit or be purchased separately) can be trailed along the bottom of the table to the edge nearest where conversations take place. It's very simple, very inexpensive, and unlikely to be discovered (unless somebody drops something and it rolls under the table).

If possible, test the location first. Put the vox recorder in the location you've selected, then place yourself in the area you expect the sound to come from, then talk in a normal voice. Turn your head in different directions and keep talking. Then play back the tape.

Remember, though, a vox recorder records *every* sound loud enough to trigger the record cycle. It's only a machine. It can't distinguish between the sound of a conversation and the sound of the radiator banging. You need to keep this in mind when selecting a location to place the device.

A working mother was worried that her son and his young friends might be using drugs during the hours between his return from school and her return from the office. She set up a vox recorder, hoping she could discern from their conversation whether they were in fact using drugs. She hid the device by taping it to the bottom of the television stand in the family room. She even tested it to make sure she could pick up a conversation that took place on the sofa, a few feet away. For some reason, it never dawned on her that her son and his friends would turn the television on. When she returned home from the office she discovered she'd only managed to record the sound effects of a video game.

Voice-activated tape recorders come in a wide variety of price categories, ranging from less than US$100 to more than US$300. You should get the best unit you can afford. If you're going to all the fuss and bother of using a vox recorder to capture conversation or other sounds, you must have a good reason; this is no time to count nickels and dimes.

Sound Amplification Dishes

The advertisements for these devices often refer to them as "bionic ears." Basically, a sound amplification dish is a very sensitive directional microphone centered in a lightweight, concave, plastic dish. The dish mimics the auricle, the fleshy part of the ear, and serves to expand the listening surface. The greater the listening surface, the more sound waves are captured, and that allows you to hear more. There's a reason some animals have such large ears. You can experience a similar effect when you cup your hand behind your ear.

The person using the sound amplification dish listens through a set of headphones. Because the dish amplifies sound, it can actually pose a risk to the user's hearing. A loud sound amplified many times can damage the ear. The headphones of most dishes, therefore, have an automatic shut-off function to protect the listener from sudden loud noises. Most dishes also include an audio jack, allowing you to record whatever it is you're listening to.

These devices are very easy to use. You just aim the dish at the person or object you want to listen to. Depending on the quality of the microphone (and some other factors discussed below) these devices can capture a conversation across the length of a football field or an argument at half a mile.

The problem with sound amplification dishes is the same problem with vox tape recorders. They can't distinguish between wanted sounds and unwanted sounds. They amplify everything. Everything, that is, in the direct line of sight of the dish. Sound waves are clearest when traveling uninterrupted in a straight direction. Objects in between the subject you're listening to and the dish tend to deflect the sound waves.

Let's say you want to hear a conversation between two people in the center of the Sheep Meadow in New York City's Central Park. With a sound amplification dish, you could easily stand in the trees that surround the meadow and listen in on the conversation. However, if you try this on a nice, sunny, weekend afternoon, the meadow will be crowded with people. The more people between you and the two people you want to listen to, the more interfering noise the dish will receive. You'll have a difficult time distinguishing between the conversation you seek and those of all the other folks out enjoying the sun.

How do you overcome this problem? One way is to get some height above the crowd. For example, if you were to climb one of the trees on the fringe of the Sheep

Meadow, you would effectively remove most of the interfering noise from the direct line of sight between the dish and the folks you want to listen to. Not that I'm suggesting anybody climb a tree on the fringe of the Sheep Meadow in Central Park; that would be certain to attract some attention—even in New York. But the principle works all the same.

It's not just detectives who use sound amplification dishes. These devices are also popular with naturalists (such as bird-watchers), hunters (who use them to locate quietly moving game animals), and sports fans (who use them to listen in on football huddles). Sound amplification dishes can be purchased through a variety of hunting or outdoor catalogs for about US$150.

Two-Way Radios

The two-way radio serves a slightly different function; it doesn't allow you to hear your subject from a distance, but it does allow you to communicate with your partners over a distance. When you're working as part of a team, that's critically important.

This is relatively ancient technology. We've been using two-way radios since before the Second World War. Obviously, the technology has improved radically over time. Modern two-way radios are smaller, lighter, and more efficient. And although they are commonly referred to as "two-way" radios, acceptable-quality units allow several users to operate on the same channel.

Two-way radios are vital equipment for detectives engaged in both mobile and stationary surveillance work. In fact, they're essential for any investigative chore that requires you to keep in touch with a partner—even if they're not used. There is a tremendous amount of comfort and confidence that comes from knowing that you can talk to a colleague if the need arises.

Depending on their quality, a two-way radio system allows detectives to communicate over a range of anywhere from a quarter-mile to five miles. The most important qualities of a two-way radio system are weight, range, and clarity. Obviously, the ideal system is one of negligible weight that allows for static-free communication at a great distance. These units are, of course, relatively expensive. It's important to decide where your priorities are before buying a two-way radio. Personally, I'm more concerned about weight and clarity than range. I'm inclined to think that if I find myself more than a mile away from my partner during a surveillance, then the situation is already falling apart.

A handy accessory for a two-way radio system is a voice activation circuit. As with a vox tape recorder, the microphone in a two-way radio with a vox circuit automatically keys open when the user speaks into it. These units usually come with a lightweight earpiece and microphone headset that's barely noticeable from more than a few feet away. A vox circuit allows for hands-free communication. That means that while you're talking with your partner you can also take notes, take photographs, eat a sandwich, or try to fold your map.

Telephone Monitor

This device allows you to turn your telephone into a microphone. You can activate it from any touch-tone telephone in the world. You simply dial your home telephone number (assuming you've attached the monitor to your home telephone) and punch in an access code using the touch-tone keypad. You can then listen in on any activity taking place within fifteen to thirty feet of the telephone. The telephone monitor, which plugs into the telephone line jack, allows you to attach up to four separate units if you have multiple telephones in different rooms through the house. You can switch between each of the four units, or listen to all four at once. The telephone monitor does not interfere with incoming or outgoing telephone calls.

These units can be found in specialty electronic goods shops or from some police and military suppliers. They cost around US$200 per unit.

MISCELLANEOUS TECHNOLOGY

There are a wide variety of high-tech tools investigators use in the course of their work. Most of them are highly specialized, and you'll never find any need for them. You won't, for example, be checking your home or apartment for bugs and wiretaps. Although some manufacturers will cheerfully sell you "home debugging" equipment, these products are basically worthless. If you suspect you're under electronic surveillance, call a qualified TSCM man (Technical Surveillance Counter Measures) to do a thorough sweep.

Nor will you be using a "bumper beeper," a radio frequency transmitter-receiver system, to tail a vehicle. Again, there are cheap vehicle tracking systems for sale through advertisements in magazines, but they are almost totally ineffective. You are no more likely to find a worthwhile vehicle tracking system sold through the back pages of a magazine than you are to find a quality video monitor or videotape recorder. These simply aren't the appropriate outlets for quality equipment.

Still, there are a few high-tech devices used by real detectives that you may find handy.

Telephone "Hold" Monitor

This odd little device, when attached to a telephone, allows the user to place the party on the other end of the line on faux hold. To the other party, it sounds as if he's been placed on hold—he hears that distinctive "dead line" sound. However, the device simply de-activates your telephone's microphone. You can hear him, but he can't hear you. This, of course, gives the other party a sense of freedom to speak his mind, either to himself or to others in the room with him. Some "hold" monitors even include a switch that allows the user to trigger a fake incoming call, giving him an excuse to place the other party on hold.

"Hold" monitors can be found in some specialty electronic goods shops. They cost approximately US$100.

Telephone Tone Decoder

This little apparatus is handy if you want to know what numbers have been called from a specific touch-tone telephone. A tone decoder will record, decode, and store up to 200 sixteen-digit telephone numbers. It displays the numbers on a small screen, rather like a caller ID box.

A tone decoder can be bought as an individual unit (approximately US$200) or as part of a long-playing tape recorder (approximately US$325). The tape recorder units often record up to five hours of conversation per cassette.

Laser Range Finder

A laser range finder is essentially an incredibly precise tape measure—only without the tape. It's surprising how often detectives need to measure distances, and most detectives carry a steel tape measure—usually a 50-foot measure, occasionally a 100-foot measure.

But a steel tape measure isn't always practical, for example, if you want to measure a distance greater than 100 feet. A laser range finder can measure distance in either feet or meters, and it does it far more quickly and with much greater accuracy. It will also give you more information than a tape measure can, such as the bearing of the target from the sighting location (for example, NNE, 25.8 degrees).

Laser range finders work by sending out a highly concentrated beam of light that reflects off the target and bounces back. Light, as Albert Einstein taught us, travels at a specific speed. By measuring the time it takes the light to travel to the target and return, the range finder can precisely measure the distance between the two.

Most laser range finders look like a monocular—a tube with an eyepiece. The user sights through the device, centers the target in the eyepiece, then pushes a button. The data (time, distance, direction) appears in the field of view. Nothing to it. A laser range finder can be found through military supply distributors and costs between US$400 and US$500.

Havelock Ellis said, "Progress is the exchange of one nuisance for another." There's a great deal of truth in that. It's important to remind ourselves not to rely too heavily on technology. If there is one thing the space shuttle Challenger disaster taught us, it's this: When technology fails, it often fails dramatically.

Having said that, only a fool refuses to use the best possible tool for the job. Technology has made the lives of investigators much easier. Use it, but don't become dependent on it. And always keep plenty of spare batteries around.

My children are growing up with computers. To them, computers are as unremarkable as the television was to me or the radio to my parents. Like computers, television and radio were revolutionary. They greatly expanded the horizons of those who used them. They made vast amounts of information available to a huge number of people. Sometimes they brought information into our homes that we didn't want. That's the risk of having access to any mass media, any impersonal communication directed at a vast audience.

But when you turn your radio or television off, it's off. All the information disappears. There is no way anybody could look at your radio or television and determine what you've been listening to or watching. When you turn off your computer, however, a great deal of information remains and may be accessed by a clever investigator.

Again, a warning. In this chapter Greg discusses some methods for gathering information by using computers. You must not use these methods to commit a crime. It is illegal to rummage around in another person's computer without their permission. It is illegal to use a password-cracking program to break into another person's private computer files. Computer crime is still crime.

R.G.

Chapter 12

GUMSHOES IN CYBERSPACE

Cyberspace. The term was coined in 1982 by an astute science-fiction writer who, at the time, didn't even own a computer. We hear the term all the time—but what *is* cyberspace? And *where* is it?

Surprisingly, cyberspace existed long before computers. It's a place that isn't really a place—at least not in a concrete sense. You can't touch it, but it is nonetheless very real in a social and technological sense.

Confused? Think of it this way. When you pick up your telephone and call your mother, where does the conversation actually take place? It doesn't happen inside your house or apartment—you're the only person there. It doesn't happen inside your telephone—that's just a tiny chunk of plastic filled with wires. The conversation takes place somewhere *out there*, in some indefinable electrical ether. You and your mother are interacting and communicating in real time across tremendous distances in this weird, ethereal electrical *place*.

That place is cyberspace. When you use your computer to access an online service (like America Online or CompuServe), when you access the Internet or the World Wide Web, your computer is connecting with another computer over telephone lines. This happens in the same *place* as your telephone conversation with your mother: cyberspace.

Here's a true thing about the investigation biz: any place people interact and share information is a place that will attract investigators. Cyberspace meets both those criteria. It doesn't matter whether you're talking about the Internet, the World Wide Web, or the Information Super-highway—they're all aspects of cyberspace. And the best tool for exploring cyberspace is a computer.

In this chapter we're going to look at computers in two ways:

- Computers as a conduit to cyberspace
- Computers as a repository of information

The distinction between the two may seem blurry at first glance, but in fact it is very definite. In the first case, we use the computer as a research tool, as a way to obtain information. In the second, we use the computer itself as a piece of evidence.

Think of the computer as your vehicle. You can use it to travel places and to explore. After you've used it for a while, you start to store stuff inside it, and that stuff can reveal something about you.

I'm going to assume that you, the reader, are computer literate, that you have some basic familiarity with computers and the Internet—otherwise this chapter would be as big as the rest of the book. Whenever possible, I will avoid highly technical and esoteric computer language. However, computers are a sophisticated technology and the language spoken in cyberspace is full of technical terms. If I use any terminology you don't understand, I suggest you use your detective skills to track down a basic computer or Internet primer. If you lack even a basic understanding of computers, then this entire chapter is a waste of your time.

THE COMPUTER AS AN INFORMATION GATHERING TOOL

The Internet is undoubtedly the single most information-rich environment that has ever existed. The depth and breadth of the information available on the Internet is staggering, and it is expanding daily. In fact, it's expanding hourly. And that's the problem. There's just too much.

Imagine the world's biggest library. Now imagine all the books, magazines, journals, maps, art galleries, reference works—the entire contents of the world's biggest library—strewn randomly on the floor. Every day a squad of madmen walk through the library removing some items, leaving others, and arbitrarily scattering the rest. That's the Internet. Almost any information you want is in there somewhere, but finding it can be difficult, and there's no guarantee that the information you find today will be in the same place tomorrow.

Obviously, I can't provide you with a complete guide to the Internet. It grows and changes far too quickly. What I can do is tell you what sorts of useful investigative information can be found and give you some idea of where it can be found.

There is a wealth of personal data on individuals stored in computer systems throughout the United States: banking records, credit histories, criminal records, medical information—all sorts of information of direct investigative use. However, you can't get to it. That sort of information is stored in secure computer data banks. Unless you are a computer hacker, it's beyond your reach.*

---

* Unfortunately, many of these so-called "secure" computers are fairly vulnerable to hackers. In order to gain access to secure computers, a hacker uses a program that locates and exploits the weaknesses in a computer's defense. These programs are not difficult to find on the Internet (although I will not tell you where to find them). A recent assault on over 200 government computers was traced to two fifteen-year-old boys in California. The program they used to break into all those computers can still be found on the Internet.

For the most part, the sorts of information you *can* gain access to through the Internet are what I call adjunct investigative information. It doesn't necessarily apply directly to your investigation, but it's associated with the investigation. Adjunct information contributes in three ways:

- It expands the scope of the investigation.
- It helps direct the course of the investigation.
- It makes the investigation easier, and therefore quicker.

How does it do this? Let me give you an example. Let's say you're sitting in front of your computer in Columbus, Ohio, and you decide you need to locate the offices of the publisher of this book, M. Evans and Company. Five minutes of "browsing" on the Web will get you their telephone number, their address in New York City, and a map showing the location of that address. In just a bit, I'll show you exactly how to do that.

Browsing the Web

How can you get access to all this information? The easiest way is through browsing the World Wide Web. The Web, in very simplistic terms, is a world-wide network of computers linked through telephone lines. Before the creation of the Web, moving around the Internet involved using a lot of obscure computer commands. The Web changed all that.

The Web is accessed through a "browser" program, which is a program that allows the user to wander through the Web without having to fuss with those obscure computer commands. The two most common browser programs are Microsoft's Internet Explorer and Netscape's Navigator. These programs make the movement from site to site on the Web as simple as clicking a button on your computer's mouse. Every Web site has a specific URL, which stands for uniform resource locator. This is essentially the address of the site. By entering the URL into your Web browser, you are simply telling your computer where to find that specific Web site.

Some Useful Web Sites

Below I've listed some of the Web sites I've found useful. These are only a fraction of the sites having adjunct investigative information. By using any of the search engines listed below and a little ingenuity, you'll discover many other useful sites.

Search Engines. A search engine is simply a program that searches the World Wide Web for sites based on key words entered by the user. There are dozens; I've only listed three.

- *Yahoo!* Perhaps the oldest and certainly one of the best Internet search engines. http://www.yahoo.com
- *AltaVista.* Easy to use and allows the user to exclude sites written in languages the user doesn't speak. http://www.altavista.digital.com
- *Lycos.* http ://www.lycos.com

Internet White/Yellow Pages. Telephone directories are important investigative tools. However, until the advent of the Internet, the only place you could find directories for a wide variety of towns and cities was at the public library—and even libraries rarely included directories from smaller towns.

The Web allows us to access white pages (individual listings), yellow pages (business listings), and even blue pages (government listings) throughout the United States. There are several such Web sites, some of which are listed below. You simply enter the name of the party you're seeking and, if possible, the city and state—and the computer does the rest (see the sidebar).

Many of these sites allow for other types of searches, such as

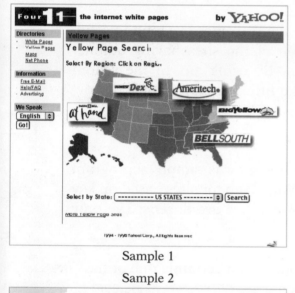

Sample 1

Sample 2

1. *A reverse search.* Enter a telephone number, and the computer will provide you with the name and address of the subscriber.

2. *A search for a person's e-mail address.* Enter the person's name, and the computer will provide you with that person's e-mail address.

3. *A reverse e-mail search.* Enter the e-mail address, and the computer will provide you with an address and telephone number.

USING THE WEB TO FIND AN ADDRESS

Earlier I used the example of a person in Ohio wanting to find the location of this book's publisher. The following example of such a search includes captured illustrations from actual Web sites.

Since publishers are businesses, I began by accessing a yellow-page Web site. As you can see in Sample 1, the site divides the U.S. into different regions. You can search by region, by state, or by city. This particular site also allows you to narrow the search by including a description of the type of business. I told the computer to look for book publishers in New York City using the name M. Evans & Company.

As seen in Sample 2, the search revealed only one match for those criteria. You'll notice that next to the address of M. Evans is a small icon in the shape of a globe. By clicking on the icon, the computer provides me with a map showing the location of the address (see Sample 3). A small "+" marks the spot. I'm not entirely satisfied with that map, so using another map site (listed under the section on maps), I enter the address for M. Evans and obtain a more detailed map (Sample 4).

The entire search took five minutes tops.

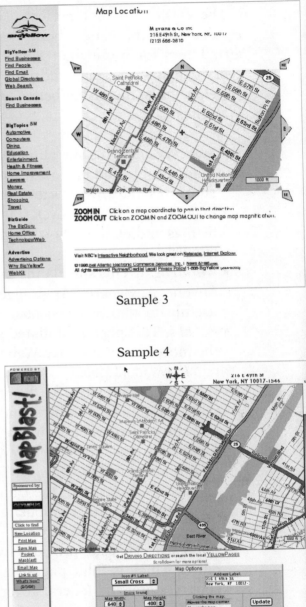

Sample 3

Sample 4

These sites are not perfect. They provide the best results when the person being sought has remained at an address for more than a year. And, of course, not everybody has an e-mail address.

Below are some of the better white- and yellow-page Web sites.

- *Switchboard.* This site allows you to locate address-es for people and businesses, as well as e-mail addresses. http://www.switchboard.com
- *Bigfoot.* This site has over 100 million white page listings and eight million e-mail addresses. http://bigfoot.com
- *WorldPages.* This site claims to "Find Anything. Anyone. Anywhere." An exaggeration, but still a useful site. http://www.worldpages.com
- *Four11.* This page is affiliated with Yahoo!, one of the more comprehensive Web search engines. http://www.four11.com
- *WhoWhere.* This site, like the others, locates add-resses, telephone numbers, and e-mail addresses. The site is also available in French, Spanish, and Japanese translations. http://www.whowhere.com
- *GTE Interactive Yellow Pages.* This site focuses on businesses throughout the United States. It's searchable by state, city, business type, or business name. http://www.bigbook.com
- *InfoSpace.* This site provides two unusual listings, one of which is "blue pages," a directory of local, county, state, and federal government agencies. http://www.infospace.com/mage/categ/bluefed.html The other is a directory of fax numbers. The fax directory also allows for a reverse search, if you know the fax number but need to know the name of the business to which it belongs. http://www.infospace.com/mage/fax.html

Map Web Sites. Although all the map sites tend to provide the same service, I've found that the maps from different sites look slightly different. I obtain maps from both of the sites listed below, and use the one that pleases me most. Both sites listed below allow the user to zoom in or out, making the map more detailed or enlarging the area to provide context.

- *Mapquest Interactive Atlas.* http://www.mapquest.com
- *Mapblast!* http://www.mapblast.com

General Information Sites. There are times during an investigation when you need to know some odd bit of information. I've worked cases in which success hinged on knowing how a furnace works, an awareness of the symptoms of temporal lobe epilepsy, the religious practices of Santeria, and crime trends in Key West, Florida. Access to general information Web sites would have made gathering such information a lot quicker.

- *Isleuth.* This is a search engine that allows you to search news agencies, Usenet discussion groups (groups of Internet users who share a common, often obscure, interest), and a variety of other information-rich sites. http://www.isleuth.com
- *The Electronic Library.* This site provides access to a huge amount of information—more than 150 newspapers, hundreds of magazines, both national and international news wires, television and radio transcripts, almanacs, and fact books. Long-term use of this site requires you to become a member and to pay a small fee. However, it offers a thirty-day free trial membership, so it's worth checking out. http://www.elibrary.com

Medical Information Sites. These sites are incredibly useful, especially in civil cases. There are times when it's vital to know the purpose of a certain pharmaceutical drug, or the diagnostic criteria for Marfan's Syndrome, or the psychological research that's been conducted on compulsive self-mutilation.

- *National Library of Medicine.* This section of the National Institutes of Health provides a massive, searchable database on every aspect of medicine. There is so much information available here that the difficulty is trying to sift through it all. http://www.nlm.nih.gov
- *RxList.* This a very useful site. It allows you to research pharmaceutical drugs by manufacturer, by brand name, and by generic name. Imagine you've been rummaging through somebody's trash, and you find an empty pill container with a label that identifies the drug as Loratadine. It's important for you to know what this drug does. RxList will help you learn that Loratadine is manufactured by Schering, and that it's the generic name of the drug Claritin, which is an antihistamine. http://www.rxlist.com

Vital Statistics Sites. Obviously, there are times when it's important for a detective to be able to obtain information on a person's vital statistics. Birth and death certificates, marriage licenses (and applications for a marriage license), and the like. It may also be important to be able to trace a person's ancestry for several generations. The Web makes these tasks easier.

- *MedAccess.* This site will provide you with the address and telephone number of vital statistics offices in cities, counties, and other local offices throughout the United States. Processing fees for obtaining copies of records are also listed. http://www.medaccess.com/address/vital_toc.htm

- *Ancestry.* This is a site for genealogists, but it includes access to databases of death registers. Very handy. http://www.ancestry.com

Legal Web Sites. A smart detective needs to keep in touch with the laws he's skirting around. There are several excellent Web sites that allow you to keep current on the law. Most are searchable by case name and subject. If you want to know the most recent court decisions pertaining to snatching somebody's trash, these sites are for you.

- *FindLaw; Internet Legal Resources.* A searchable database of civil and criminal law. Easy to use. http://www.findlaw.com
- *USSC+.* This site labels itself "the best digital resource for United States Supreme Court research." And that may be accurate. It not only provides an easily searchable database of decisions dating back to 1953, it also includes all of the Supreme Court decisions handed down during the current term. If that's not enough, it gives you information about the workings of the Court and its justices. http://www.usscplus.com

U.S. Government Web Sites. The government of the United States collects huge amounts of data, a great deal of which can be useful to a clever investigator.

- *Securities and Exchange Commission.* This site will allow you to retrieve publicly available filings submitted to the Securities and Exchange Commission from January 1994 to the present. Now, what use is that? The filings are jammed with useful information, such as the business and home addresses of the owner and officers of a corporation, statements about changes that benefit corporate officers, and financial and stock options available and exercised by the officers and owners. Handy information to have. http://www.sec.gov/cgi-bin/srch-edgar

- *U.S. Census Bureau.* This site provides statistics and census data. This may not sound useful at first, but it can provide a great deal of contextual information. If you have to interview a witness who lives in, say, Dubuque, Iowa, it's helpful to know something about the people of Dubuque before you arrive. It's nice to know that only 78 percent of the folks living in Dubuque graduated from high school, and that only 17 percent graduated from college. It helps to know that 86 percent of the people living there are under sixty-five years of age, that the mean per capita income is just under US$19,000, and the per capita amount of savings is around US$11,000. It's wonderful background information. http://www.census.gov

Investigative Equipment Sites. Need to buy a night vision device or a laser range finder? Want to know more about wiretapping and bugging? Interested in the more arcane aspects of radio frequency vehicle tracking devices? The following sites can be a valuable resource for investigative tools and information:

- *SWS Security.* These folks manufacture electronic surveillance, intelligence gathering, and radio communications systems. Their site also includes arti-

cles on electronic surveillance, night vision equipment, and vehicle-tracking systems.
http://www.swssec.com/index.html

- *InSight Police Supplier.* Most of the items offered on this site are of little use to the amateur detective, but for those of you who want a heavy flashlight like those carried by police officers, this is the place to shop. http://in-sight.policesupplier.com
- *Granite Island Group; Technical Surveillance Counter Measures.* Again, this site is directed more toward the professional investigator, but it offers a wealth of information on wiretapping and bugging, including photos of the equipment used to do it. http://www.tscm.com/threatvid.html

Miscellaneous Web Sites. One of the things that makes detective work so interesting is the variety. You never know what sorts of things you'll need to know to resolve a case. You may need the names of all the ships having Panamanian registry that docked in San Diego last week. You may need to know if a person living in Illinois is listed as a deadbeat dad in Arizona. You may need to discover if a person is a licensed pilot in England.

The sites listed below offer a highly diverse fund of information that may, or may not, be useful to detectives.

- *Black Book Online.* This site refers to itself as "A Guide to Free Web Based Database Searches For PI's." It does include a variety of searchable databases, including registries of deadbeat dads from the various states. http://www.crimetime.com/online.html
- *Military City.* This site is designed for active-duty and retired military personnel. It can be helpful in locating the bases where current members of the

military are stationed. http://www.militarycity.com

- *AmeriCom Long Distance Area Decoder.* This site is useful for finding the location of a given area code. Although that information is also available in the hard-copy telephone directory, new area codes are being created all the time. This site is usually more up-to-date than the phone book. http://decoder.americom.com

- *Informus Corp.* This is a site developed by a company that provides employee screening information. Although you have to pay for most of the information they have available, they include a small program that allows the user to verify his or her own Social Security number. That means you can also verify if somebody else is using a fake Social Security number. The program informs you if the number is authentic and also provides you with the state that issued the number as well as the approximate date it was issued. http://www.informus.com/ssnlkup.html

- *Certified Pilot Database.* This site includes a searchable database with a listing of approximately 600,000 licensed pilots, both for the U.S. and the U.K. There are also links that allow you access to an aviation medical examiners database, National Transportation Safety Bureau accident reports, and federal aviation regulations. The URL is unusually long (the hyphen at the end of the first line should be typed). http://www1.drive.net/evird.acgi$pass*42435!_h-www.landings.com/_landings/pages/search.html.

Obviously, the Web sites listed in this chapter are only a surface scan of all the available Web sites that are useful to investigators. Thousands of new sites are created every week, most of which are entirely useless.

Still, there are gems hidden amid the trash. For that reason, one of the most useful sites on the Web is the following:

- *Yahoo!—What's New?* This site lists hundreds of new Web sites categorized by topic, with each topic having several subcategories. It's updated daily. http://www.yahoo.com/new

Even if you don't intend to actually be your own detective, the World Wide Web is an amazing source of information. I advise everybody to get wired and to check it out.

THE COMPUTER AS A SOURCE OF INFORMATION

Computer technology changes at a head-spinning pace. Every computer owner has known the frustration of discovering the state-of-the-art computer he or she recently bought is considered out-of-date within a couple of months.

Although the technology shifts every few months, people tend to keep using computers the same way and for the same purposes. Much of what a person uses a computer for ends up stored in the computer's memory. If you have access to another person's computer (and are willing to violate the owner's privacy) you can learn a lot about that person. Home computers often contain tax information, credit card numbers, bank statements, medical records, addresses, and other information about a person's family and friends.

Again, I have to assume a basic level of computer literacy here. If you lack all understanding of computers, then you're wasting your time.

Computer Snooping

The most obvious, as well as the easiest, way to commit computer snooping is simply to start rummaging through the owner's stored files. This is best done by starting individual programs (a word processor, for example, or a banking or tax program) and using the program to call up the files associated with that program. Then it's just a matter of reading, copying, or printing the material.

Computer programs often make this very easy. For the user's convenience, many programs maintain a list of the most recently used (MRU) files—handy for the user, *very* handy for an investigator interested in what the user has been working on. Eliminating MRU lists is a simple process, but most users never bother.

You'd think deleting a file would make it safe from prying eyes. Wrong. Many computer operating systems simply move a "deleted" file to a recycling bin. All the investigator needs to do is to access the recycling bin. (There's usually a trash can icon that, when clicked on, takes the user directly to the recycling bin.) There, the "deleted" file can easily be returned to its original program.

And if a file has been deleted from the recycling bin? No problem. In order to protect inexperienced computer users from making an irreversible mistake (accidentally deleting a needed file), most computer operating systems include an easy-to-use "undelete" program. It lists all the "deleted" files and offers to undelete them.*

---

* Even if the undelete program says the "deleted" file can't be recovered, it usually can be. A computer-savvy detective who is rummaging through a personal computer will bring along more sophisticated undelete software. The only way to be certain that a file won't be accessed is to remove the hard drive, surround it with magnets, then bury it in a fifty-five-gallon drum of nuclear waste. Well, maybe I'm exaggerating, but not by much.

Many computer programs permit users to guard their data through the use of passwords. A password is a series of letters and/or numbers the user must type in before the program will allow access to the data. However, surprisingly few computer users actually bother using passwords on their home computers. What should you do if you encounter a program that is protected by a password? The decent thing to do is to give up. Turn off the computer, and go have a beer. However, if you're already snooping through somebody's files, we'll assume you're managing to keep a tight rein on your sense of decency. In that case, you should give some thought to cracking the password.

Cracking Passwords. Surprisingly, most of the people who bother using passwords to protect their files don't bother to concoct a suitable password. People often use their names, or the names of somebody close to them, or a pet's name, or some variation of those. For example, if the computer owner has a dog named Spike, he may use that as his password. If he's clever (or thinks he is) he may substitute a number for a similar letter. So instead of "Spike," his password might be "Sp1ke." Birthdates are also popular passwords. It's always a good idea to try a few of the obvious passwords and their variations before moving on to more sophisticated techniques.

Another simple idea is merely to look around the computer. It's appalling how many people, fearful they'll forget their password, will write it down and slip it under the keyboard or in a nearby desk drawer. A quick search of the area within a hand's reach of the computer will often reveal the password. I've even known people who have written their password on a Post-it and put it on the side of the computer.

Even when computer owners are more cautious, it's not that difficult to crack their passwords. Most people

BUILDING THE
PERFECT PASSWORD

Since I've spent so much time showing you how people crack passwords, it seems only right that I also show you how to choose a password that *will* protect your data. A good password is one that is totally random. Here's how to create one.

First, remember that most password programs allow users to select a password up to 16 characters in length. Now, take a dictionary. Close your eyes, and open it up to a random page. With your eyes still closed, put your finger on a random spot on this page. I just selected "cube." Now, repeat the process. I selected "posy." Now combine the two words. Cubeposy. Deliberately misspell one of the words. Kubeposy. Now add a three digit number. Kubeposy438. Finally, alter some of the letters into numerical characters. For example, exchange the "e" for a "3" and the "o" for a "0". That gives you Kub3p0sy438.

No password cracking program will ever crack that. And although it looks odd (which is a benefit), the process you used to create it actually makes it easily memorable.

But you're still not entirely safe. Remember, *never* write your password down. And *never* give it anybody else.

simply choose a random English-language word for their password. That sounds safe enough, doesn't it? After all, how likely is it that a stranger will guess your password is "subway"? Highly unlikely. People who are serious about cracking passwords, however, don't spend much time guessing. Instead, they'll run a password-cracking program that tries every single word in the dictionary. On a fast computer, that will only take a few minutes.

Sound improbable? Password-cracking programs are easily available on the World Wide Web. In less than five minutes of searching the Web, I found password-cracking programs that test for potential passwords in the following ways: (1) by common surnames; (2) by using a dictionary of given names (male and female); (3) by names of asteroids; (4) by biological terms; (5) by names of cartoon characters; (6) by names of famous people, places, and things; (7) by names from the King James Bible; (8) by names from the Koran; (9) by names of famous movie characters and movie titles; (10) by names of legends and myths; (11) by names and words associated with Monty Python; (12) by names in Shakespeare; (13) by names of sports figures and teams; (14) by "obscene" words; and (15) by words, names of characters, ships, species, and items from *Star Trek*.

Armed with such tools, very few "password-protected" files will stay that way. And here's another alarming fact: Most computer users choose the same password for all their programs. That means if you find the password for a person's banking program, you most likely have the password for all their other protected programs.

Where can you get copies of these password-cracking programs? I won't give out that information. Still, if you can use the simple Web browsing tools discussed earlier, it shouldn't take you more than a quarter of an hour to find a Web site that supplies such programs.

More sophisticated computer investigators can, using the Web, also locate sites that will provide detailed information on how to bypass security systems. I took the following introduction from one such site:

> *This file describes how to break-in to an IBM-compatible PC from the outside in, and how to bypass most software-based security measures.*

Again, I will not provide you with the URLs for such sites, but they are quite easy to locate.

Cookies

Cookies. Sounds harmless, doesn't it? Almost cheerful. Most people would be charmed by the idea that their personal computer has cookies hidden away inside it. For an investigator, however, cookies can be very revealing.

What are cookies? A cookie is a small piece of information that's sent to your Web browser when you access a particular Web site. Let's say, for example, I want to look for a book to buy from the online bookstore

Amazon.com. When I access their Web site, their computer automatically sends my computer a cookie. This tiny bit of information is saved on my hard drive. The next time I return to the Amazon.com site, some of that cookie—that stored information—is sent back to their Web server.

Why does this happen? One reason is marketing. Cookies are used to personalize Web interactions. For example, when I access Amazon.com, their opening Web page will say "Welcome Back Greg Fallis!" The site will then recommend books I might be interested in based on my previous purchases.

All of this exchange of information is invisible to the computer user. However, hidden away somewhere on your hard drive is a file named "Cookies" and it contains a list of Web sites you've visited recently.* By copying your cookie list and visiting those sites an investigator can gather some idea of your interests. A cookie for an online bookstore may be revealing; a cookie for an online sex club is even more so.

In addition, some of the more advanced Web sites require you to use a password. And, as we've already discussed, people tend to use the same password for every program and computer application.

As you've probably figured out by now, computers are wonderful tools for investigators. They are also repositories of highly personal information about their owners. A good detective should know how to use the tool, how to exploit the weaknesses of computers owned by other people, and how to keep his own computer secure.

---

* The two most common Web browsers store cookie files in different places. Netscape Navigator stores all cookies in a file named cookies.txt. The file is in the same directory where Navigator is installed. Microsoft's Internet Explorer keeps each cookie in a separate file in the c:\windows\cookies directory.

Computer security issues change as quickly as the rest of the computer industry. The only way to stay current is, that's right, to use the Web to access computer security sites.

I confess. The first time I met a private detective, I asked a lot of these questions, too. We've been conditioned to think of detectives and detective work as glamorous in a seedy sort of way. We want them to be what they are in the movies, and we're disappointed to learn they don't act like their celluloid counterparts.

A few private detectives do take on the trappings of the fictional detective. The shoulder holster, the trenchcoat, the snappy patter, and the hard-boiled cynicism. These guys are rarely any good. They're too busy living the fantasy.

I was at a glitzy party one night when an attractive woman asked Greg what he did for a living. He said he worked for the post office. You could almost see the woman recoil. After a few minutes of polite conversation, she wandered off to find somebody more interesting.

R.G.

Chapter 13

THE TEN MOST COMMON QUESTIONS

When people learn you're a private detective, they tend to have one of two reactions. Either they look at you like you're an ax murderer and shy away, or they begin to ask you questions.

I've come to prefer the ax murderer response. Not because I'm ashamed of what I do, but because I can anticipate what the questions will be. They're almost always the same. They're good questions, for the most part. It's just that I'd like to answer some new ones.

It was pointed out to me that, although I've addressed some of the more esoteric issues about being a detective, I've ignored the more common questions. So here they are. The ten most common questions. Now when people ask me these questions, I can tell them to read the book.

Is it dangerous?

No, not really. When you compare it to being a police officer, or a fire fighter, or operating a convenience store in a bad neighborhood, being a private detective is almost safe.

On the other hand, it ain't no walk in the park. Only a fool would tell you there's no need to be cautious. It's an intrusive occupation. The entire purpose of the job is to meddle in the lives of other people. They tend to resent that. And there are always folks who, perhaps, aren't socialized as well as the rest of us, folks who don't handle their anger very well. It can be a problem.

I once had the bad luck to irritate a group of bikers. It's a long, twisted story revolving around the sale of cocaine, a material witness to a homicide, and a house stuffed full of stolen electronic equipment. We had a little misunderstanding, which resulted in one of the bikers getting arrested. The following evening, his buddies spoke with me in an alley, threatening me with something unpleasant involving the sexual knowledge of a long lead pipe.

Nothing really bad happened, of course. It rarely does. I've been pushed around a bit, threatened with alarming regularity, spat on, cursed at, and generally treated like a leper. But, for the most part, people seem to be reluctant to actually lay hands on a private detective. A fact for which I am profoundly grateful.

Given the chance, I'm a coward. People can insult me all they want, as long as they keep their hands and lead pipes to themselves. That old sticks-and-stones aphorism is true.

Dogs, on the other hand, were put on earth by Satan to plague detectives. Don't misunderstand me, I dearly love dogs. When I'm not working. But if I had to make a list of things that pose a threat to the detective's life and limb, dogs would be right at the top. Dogs would rank far ahead of drug-crazed bikers, irate husbands, and psychopathic killers. The only blood I've ever shed in the line of duty was the result of a fuss I had with a rottweiler.

Do you carry a gun?

No. Guns cause more problems than they solve. Introduce a gun into a potentially volatile situation, and it escalates all out of proportion. Guns make people irrational.

As a defensive weapon, guns are vastly overrated. People have this idea (another gift of television) that all you have to do is whip out a gun and people become very cooperative. Real life isn't that neat. Show an angry man a gun, and he might just decide to make you use it. Or he might try to take it away from you. And he might succeed.

Most of the ugly situations I've been in have taken place at very close quarters. Close enough to put hands on somebody. At that range, guns are as dangerous to you as they are to the person you intend to shoot. (I'm assuming you know enough not to draw a weapon unless you plan to shoot somebody.) You reach for a gun, the person grabs you, and you're as likely to shoot yourself as him. From a distance of five feet or more, I suppose you could draw your weapon and shoot your intended victim to your heart's content. But inside of three feet—and that's where most of the action takes place—you stand a good chance of damaging yourself.

If I'd tried to pull a gun on the bikers I mentioned earlier, they'd have followed through on their threat to do something rude with that lead pipe—assuming I didn't shoot myself trying to get the weapon out.

Anybody who wants to shoot me will have to bring his own gun. Besides, guns are heavy and uncomfortable to wear.

A detective's best weapon is his wits. You can talk or charm your way out of most trouble. Of course, charm is worthless against a rottweiler. (If you're not familiar with the breed, a rottweiler is a large, lovely dog that, when angered, resembles Mike Tyson in an amphetamine rage.) A small nuclear device might be effective against a rottweiler.

When confronted by those bikers, I apologized. I groveled, and I whimpered. That was what they wanted. It made them feel manly and tough, and it got me out of the alley intact. We were both happy. The course of the investigation didn't change. And that's what's important.

You have to have your priorities straight.

Are you ever bothered by the ethics?

Sometimes. Being a professional snoop isn't always pleasant. Manipulating people, stretching the truth, sneaking around—my momma didn't raise me to behave that way. So, of course it bothers me.

But people don't consult a private detective unless they're seriously troubled by something. They desperately want answers. The answers they get may not be the ones they want, but at least they have them. Ignorance isn't always bliss; sometimes it's torture.

Picture a fifty-five-year-old woman, a housewife who has never been employed and has no marketable skills. Her children have grown up and moved away. She has no family in the area. She suspects her husband is having an affair and may be planning to divorce her. She needs to *know*. She has to protect herself. And she can't do it alone.

This is one of the very few occupations in which moral issues aren't abstract. Concrete moral decisions have to made on a daily basis. The choices are rarely clear; at times the decision isn't between right and wrong, but between which action is least wrong. That's part of what makes it interesting.

Is it like it is on television/in the movies/in novels?

Never. Well, almost never. I've never been *hired* to find a killer, but I have helped clear a man of a murder charge by finding the real murderer. I've never been embroiled in a case involving obscure South American poisons, but I have worked on a bow-and-arrow murder. I've never been asked to locate a missing heiress or a kidnapped princess, but I have been asked to find a centerfold model for a famous men's magazine who disappeared with a great deal of jewelry belonging to her lover's wife. Nobody has ever tried to kill me, at least not in a work-related incident. I've never been hired to protect any-body, although I was once approached by a woman who wanted me to terrorize her husband. And I've never driven a bright red Ferrari. Never. But I'd like to.

It can't be like the movies or television or novels. Fiction has to make sense; by the end of the story all the loose ends have to be tied up. Unfortunately, real life is under no obligation to be tidy.

How did you become a detective/How can I become a detective?

Believe it or not, I became a detective by answering an advertisement in the newspaper. The public defenders were looking for an investigator. I knew criminals; I'd been working as a counselor in a women's prison. I knew violence; I'd been a medic in the military. I got the job and got my license. The rest, as they say, is history.

How *you* can become a detective depends on where you live. Each state has its own regulations regarding the licensing of private detectives. In some states you have to pass a test, in others you need a minimum of two years experience working under another detective's license, in still other states all you need to do is fill out an application and find a company to bond you. Getting bonded is often the most difficult task. Bonding compa-nies are accustomed to all sorts of quacks coming in with visions of Sam Spade dancing around their heads.

How do you get clients?

If you're good (or lucky), you develop a reputation in the legal community. Lawyers recommend you to other lawyers. Clients recommend you to other clients. Word gets around. A few big cases help. I was lucky enough to get involved in a nasty murder early in my career.

But when most people need a private detective, they look for one the same way they look for a plumber. They look in the yellow pages. Detectives advertise just like plumbers. And often work in the same milieu.

Can you make any money at it?

If you have a good reputation, yes. If you're willing to accept ugly cases, yes. If you don't mind immersing yourself in the crises of others, yes. If you have a license, yes, you can make money. Not a vulgar amount, but a decent wage. Well, that's not quite true. It's possible to earn a vulgar amount, but that usually involves a corporate clientele or an obscenely rich client who is extremely publicity-shy.

But nobody should get in the business expecting to make a lot of money.

Why do you do it?

Well, I don't anymore (although Ruth Greenberg continues to practice law). Since the first edition of this book was published, I have gone on to other things. But I can still tell you why I did it, why I engaged in detective work.

I did it because I liked it. It suited me. I liked being on the streets late at night, when all the good people are at home in bed. I liked the people I met and worked with—the lawyers, the criminals, the cops, the desperate people.

I liked the ambiguity and the uncertainty. I liked not knowing exactly what was going to happen next. I liked the intensity, the way everything you did mattered. I liked being able to sleep late (which is one reason I specialized in criminal work; criminals keep later hours). I liked the fact that every case offered the opportunity to see and learn something new. I even liked the fact that, after learning something I felt certain was important, I wasn't always sure what it was I'd learned.

I once saw a man kill a kitten. He just killed it, for no apparent reason. He was sitting in the back of a pick-up truck, holding it cupped in his hands. Suddenly he just twisted its head, snapped its neck. He looked at it for a moment, then tossed the limp little body out of the truck. I *knew* I'd had some elemental glimpse into the human condition, maybe something to do with why some people end up as serial killers. Something horrible. I'm not sure what it was, I'm not sure what it meant. But I know that even now, years after it happened, it haunts me.

I didn't like the ugliness, the suffering. I didn't like the way people sometimes treat each other, the way people who once loved each other turn spiteful and bitter.

But every so often, amid all the cruelty, there were small, exquisite acts of tenderness. There were moments so touching that you're never quite the same afterwards. I was investigating an assault case during the holiday season and had to interview a young couple who'd witnessed the assault. They were living in a tiny, underheated apartment and were so poor they couldn't afford to buy a Christmas tree. But somebody had discarded the sawn-off end of one, a stump about six inches tall with maybe a half dozen branches leafing out of it.

They'd brought this stump into their apartment and dec-
orated it with popcorn and cranberries strung on
thread. They were sort of embarrassed by the tree
stump, as if I would judge them by their poverty. And at
the same time, they were proud of it, and of themselves.
They were making their first Christmas together.

They were young and poor and probably borderline
retarded. And they were so absolutely in love with each
other. Seeing the way they treated each other, the care they
each took to ensure the other was happy, was like a gift.

It made redemption seem possible.

Why did you stop doing it?

Now, that's a more difficult question. I could give you any
number of answers, most of which would be at least partially true. But the simple fact is that I had burned out.
Not just once, but several times. Meddling in the lives of
other folks is interesting (in a warped way, admittedly),
but it's also wearing. After seven years of almost daily
encounters with violence, infidelity, suspicion, crime,
deceit, and tragedy, I finally decided I'd had enough.

I can even tell you the moment I made the decision.
Earlier in the book I mentioned the cranky old woman
who had managed a small market near my office. We
were never friends. She was always ill-tempered, her
arthritic dog smelled, and her cats were as fussy as she
was. But I knew her, and over time we had managed to
carve out a sort of nonadversarial relationship. Then
one winter day both she and that fat, old dog were
stabbed to death during a burglary of the store and I was
assigned to help defend one of the folks charged with
the crime. Several days later, while shooting photographs of the crime scene, I managed to get some of
the old woman's dried blood in the grooves of my sneak-

ers. As I walked back to my office, I noticed I was leaving a coppery-colored trail in the snow behind me. It was the old woman's blood. Or it might have been the old dog's blood. It didn't make any difference. For a moment I was overwhelmed by the horror of it.

That's when I made the decision. I rinsed the soles of my sneakers in a small pool of melting snow and decided I should do something else for a while.

It took me a few months to arrange, but I decided to take a year off from investigating. That year has just continued to stretch out. I continue to spend most of my time dealing with crime and criminality, but no longer in the trenches.

I miss it sometimes. I miss it the way an amputee misses a gangrenous leg that had to be removed. I know I'm better off without it, but I still miss it. I miss those late nights, I miss all the weird people (criminals and lawyers alike), I miss the comradery that exists during an intense investigation or a criminal trial, I miss the excitement. It was, without a doubt, the most fun and the most important work I've ever done or am ever likely to do.

Can you teach me how to do it?

We just did.

APPENDIX A

Social Security Numbers

The first three digits of a person's Social Security number (SSN) are the area number. For numbers assigned prior to 1973, the area number indicates the specific Social Security office from which the card was issued, which generally corresponds to a particular state. Since 1973, certain blocks of numbers have been allocated to each state, as listed below. Population shifts to the South and Southwest have forced the Social Security Administration to allocate some numbers out of sequence.

The middle two digits are referred to as the group number. They have no geographical significance. They simply break the SSN into conveniently sized blocks for use in internal operations and order of issuance.

The last four digits are the serial number. This represents a straight numerical series of numbers from 0001-9999 within each group.

The current nine-digit number provides almost one billion individual Social Security numbers. Only about one-third of the possible SSNs have been issued.

001–003	New Hampshire
004–007	Maine
008–009	Vermont
010–034	Massachusetts
035–039	Rhode Island
040–049	Connecticut
050–134	New York
135–158	New Jersey
159–211	Pennsylvania
212–220	Maryland
221–222	Delaware

223–231	Virginia
232–236	West Virginia
237–246	North Carolina
247–251	South Carolina
252–260	Georgia
261–267	Florida
268–302	Ohio
303–317	Indiana
318–361	Illinois
362–386	Michigan
387–399	Wisconsin
400–407	Kentucky
408–415	Tennessee
416–424	Alabama
425–428, 587	Mississippi
429–432	Arkansas
433–439	Louisiana
440–448	Oklahoma
449–467	Texas
468–477	Minnesota
478–485	Iowa
486–500	Missouri
501–502	North Dakota
503–504	South Dakota
505–508	Nebraska
509–515	Kansas
516–517	Montana
518–519	Idaho
520–524	Colorado
525, 585	New Mexico
526–527	Arizona
528–529	Utah
530	Nevada
531–539	Washington
540–544	Oregon
545–573	California
574	Alaska
575–576	Hawaii
577–579	Washington, D.C.
580	U.S. Virgin Islands
581–582	Puerto Rico
583–584, 586	Guam, U.S. Samoa, and other Pacific Territories

APPENDIX B

Sam Spade Conjuror's Kit

This is my term for the kit of useful tools and accessories carried by most detectives. Every detective has individual needs, and no two kits will be exactly alike.

The kit should always be kept handy. I keep mine in my car, in an old medical supply bag.

- *Steel tape measure.* A 100-foot steel tape measure is best; a 50-foot tape isn't always long enough, and there's little difference between the size of a 100-foot tape and 50-foot tape. Steel is best. Plastic gets brittle in the cold and shatters if cars drive over it. (Don't laugh—it's happened to me too many times.) Of course, a laser range finder is a nice measuring tool as well.
- *Voice-activated tape recorder.* Include plenty of new, blank tapes. Don't try to re-record too often; the sound quality degrades.
- *35-mm camera.* Take along with the appropriate lenses, flash, extra film, tripod (or collapsing monopod), and, of course, extra batteries.
- *Two flashlights.* A mini-light for those occasions that demand discretion, and a large five-cell steel light for power and whacking rottweilers. I recommend a Mag-lite. Again, include extra batteries.
- *Tape.* Scotch tape, for attaching messages. (I've also used it surreptitiously to tape a thread or hair across a door to see if anybody has left or entered since I was last there.) Also, take duct tape, because almost anything can be repaired with duct tape.
- *Survival tool.* That's the generic name for those multi-purpose tools that look like folding pliers. They generally con-

tain everything from a knife blade and a wire-stripper to various screwdriver blades.

- *Magnifying lens.* You rarely need one, but when you do, you really do. I also carry a small jeweler's loupe.
- *Other stuff.* This means pencils, pens, string, breath mints, paper clips, and the like.
- *Extra batteries.* Carry extra batteries for everything. And replace them once a year, even if they haven't been used. You can't afford to have a total battery failure.

APPENDIX C

Adopted Children and Birth Parents

It has always been difficult for adopted children to locate their birth parents and, conversely, for birth parents to search for the children they gave up for adoption. The process is deliberately difficult, which is as it should be. Women who place their children for adoption usually have good reasons for doing so. Their privacy should be respected. However, even in those circumstances where both parent and child wanted to find each other, bureaucratic barriers often made it difficult.

The emergence of the World Wide Web has changed that to some degree. The Web's simplicity of use, wide availability of access, and sheer reach have made it possible for numerous adopted children and birth parents to find each other.

Indeed, there is something of a cottage industry of individuals and agencies that exist solely to help adopted children and birth parents find each other. Sadly, some of those who advertise their services on the Web merely use the needs of birth parents and adopted children as an opportunity to victimize the desperate.

There are several adoptee search services available on the Web. Most of them are linked to each other (that is, each Web site contains an icon that leads the user to a related site). Some sites are national registries, some are confined to a particular state, and some are international. (With the rise of adoptions from foreign countries, the latter is becoming an increasingly important area of research for adopted children.)

These reunion sites work by maintaining registers of adoptees and birth parents. Each party posts the sort of information the other will need to find him or her. Much of that information is personal (see the warning on the next page).

Three Web sites help reunite adopted children and birth parents. Each of these sites is linked with other adoption-reunion sites.

Remember, however, that these sites are primarily successful only when both parties—adoptee and birth parent—are searching for each other. If only one of the parties is involved in the search, the chances for success plummet.

And be warned: There is a good chance that if you post information about yourself on one of these sites, you will receive unsolicited e-mail from search agencies.

- *Adoptee Search Center.*
  http://members.aol.com/MavsIce/index.html
- *Reunion Registry.* This site calls itself "The World's Largest Free Mutual-Consent Reunion Registry on the Internet." It's not just for adoptees, but for anybody looking to be reunited with somebody else—old friends, lost loves, and the like. http://www.reunionregistry.com
- *Reunions Online.* This site also gives realistic warnings to its users, which I find very responsible. http://www.absnw.com/reunions

---

Public Information Sources
(Other Than the World Wide Web)

These are some of the more common sources of public information. For the computer literate, there are also a variety of World Wide Web sites than can facilitate your search for this information. The list of abbreviations appears at the end of this section.

Information sought: Name
Information source: TD, CD, VR, CCCF, TA, CR, CCVS, UC, DMV, SOSCD
Notes: A legal change in name will be recorded in the county recorder's office. Businesses often operate under a pseudonym referred to as a "DBA" (doing business as); owner's names can be verified by SOCSD.

Information sought: Address
Information source: TD, CD, PO, TC, VR, TA, CR, UC, DMV
Notes: The post office is no longer required to make forwarding addresses public.

Information sought: Date of birth
Information source: CCVS, CCML, DMV, PL(NM), NM
Notes: If you have a general idea of a subject's date of birth, search the birth announcements in old newspapers.

Information sought: Description
Information source: DMV
Notes: You can also obtain blood types from birth certificates.

Information sought: Employment
Information source: VR, CD
Notes: Rental and lease agreements commonly require the renter to list his or her place of employment.

Information sought: Marital status
Information source: CCCF, CCML, CD, CR, NM, PL(NM)
Notes: Be sure to check for applications for marriage licenses as well as for licenses themselves. Not every license applied for is used.

Information sought: Prior address
Information source: TC, UC
Notes: Old TDs and CDs are often stored at public libraries.

Information sought: Vehicle information (owner, description, vehicle identification number, license number)
Information source: DMV
Notes: Each vehicle has a unique vehicle identification number (VIN), which is a code identifying the vehicle's make, model, and year of manufacture.

Information sought: Information regarding parents of the subject
Information source: CCML, CCVS, CR, SD
Notes: Birth certificates also record the occupations of both birth parents.

Information sought: Information regarding the children of the subject
Information source: CCCF, CCVS, SD, CD

Notes: Although children are not free of the grasp of bureaucracy, they are generally more loosely held. Little information is available (and, let's face it, little information is important) about infants.

Information sought: Divorce information
Information source: CCCF, PL(NM)
Notes: In addition to the date of dissolution, the divorce decree will also include such information as the disposal of community property, names and ages of children, income of the parent required to pay support or alimony, places of employment, and new addresses.

Information sought: Business information
Information source: BBB, COC, SOSCD, PL, SEC, CCCF, CCCrF
Notes: The SEC is a federal agency that receives reports from thousands of corporations. It publishes an annual directory (also available online) that provides information about each of these companies. The public library will probably have a copy of at least one register of corporations (*Dun & Bradstreet*, *Standard & Poor's*, or *Moody's*) that lists subsidiary corporations. The CCCF and CCCrF will have details regarding civil suits and criminal cases involving corporations. The BBB will provide information regarding the reputation of a local business.

Information sought: Information on a deceased person
Information source: CR, ME, PL(NM), NM, PC
Notes: Available information includes place and cause of death, survivors, disposition and value of estate, and veteran status.

Information sought: Information on property
Information source: CR, PC, TA, CA, CCCF, BD
Notes: These sources deal mainly with real property, such as land and houses, as well as any improvements made to such property.

Information sought: Civil legal proceedings
Information source: CCCF, NM
Notes: By consulting the civil files, you can also discover the
names of the lawyers representing the parties involved.

Information sought: Physician information
Information source: PL(AMD), SLB
Notes: Physicians are licensed by the state in which they practice. Consult the proper licensing board to learn about
complaints.

Information sought: Airplane and boat ownership
Information source: FAA, DMV
Notes: Information on ships can be obtained through *Lloyd's
Register of Shipping and Yachts.*

Information sought: Information on tavern owners
Information source: ABCB
Notes: Information includes the home address of the bar
owner, as well as his telephone number, DBA, and fingerprints.

ABCB—Alcoholic Beverage Control Board
BBB—Better Business Bureau
BD—building department
CA—county auditor
CD—city directory
CCCF—county clerk, civil files
CCCrF—county clerk, criminal files
CCML—county clerk, marriage license
CCVS—county clerk, vital statistics
COC—chamber of commerce
CR—county recorder
DMV—Department of Motor Vehicles
FAA—Federal Aviation Administration
ME—medical examiner
NM—newspaper "morgue"
PC—probate court
PL—public library
PL(AMD)—public library (*American Medical Dictionary*)
PL(NM)—public library (newspaper "morgue")
PO—post office
SD—school department
SEC—Securities and Exchange Commission
SLB—State Licensing Board
SOSCD—Secretary of State, corporate division
TA—tax assessor
TC—telephone company
TD—telephone directory
UC—utility companies (gas, water, electricity)
VR—voter registration

Now you know what to look for. You know what to do. Keep your eye on the rearview mirror at all times. Drive rental cars. Burn your trash. Lock your mailbox. Buy property under a false name. Register your car under your sister's name. Don't marry. Don't go to the doctor. Pay cash. Get curtains, and keep them closed. Change your clothes often. Affect a limp. Don't visit your mother. Write nothing down. Smash your computer. Speak to no one. Give nothing away.

Or . . . make your life an open book and live naked and unafraid.

R.G.